D0045504

"Dan is a legend. Growing up in Pittsburgh during the 80s and 90s, it was all about MTV and Rock n' Jock. My friends and I always loved that Dan flew his home town flag proudly and I always paid attention and was proud whenever he showed up on TV. He always looked like he was having so much fun and after reading Step Off! *apparently, he still is!"*

—Joe Manganiello, actor and producer

"Dan has always been an intelligent, cool and fun guy. Step Off! *allows you to take a front row seat to Dan's hilarious, insightful, and wisdom filled account of how he navigates the ups and downs of Hollywood, life and fatherhood."*

—Heather Dubrow. TV personality, author and host of *Heather Dubrow's World* podcast.

"When I was an athlete in college I and all my friends wanted to be Dan Cortese. He was the coolest guy with the greatest job living the dream. We knew the guy we saw on tv but years later after getting to know Dan and reading his book I discovered that the real Dan Cortese is even better—deeper, more reflective, funny, loving and spiritual. Step Off! *is one of the best books I've read in a long time. I loved learning how Dan became the icon he is but my favorite part was learning about the man he's become. Read this book! You will love it!"*

—Jon Gordon, best-selling author of *The Energy Bus* and *Training Camp.*

"Congrats to Dan on writing this book! As a fellow MTV alum, I loved hearing about his journey and life lessons with all the 80s and 90s references sprinkled in —those were the days even if some of the outfits are regrettable! We've known each other both as MTV neophytes and later as Malibu parents. What has always been apparent is Dan's penchant for fun and his "why not?" approach to life. Thanks again for reminding us that the glass is half full and giving us some great laughs along the way."

—Cindy Crawford, model and entrepreneur

"*Heartfelt, hilarious, reflective and on point,* Step Off! *moved me from start to finish! As a brand new father, the message and timing of this book could not be more divine . . . its spiritual without being 'spiritual' it provokes without being preachy and Cortese's positive outlook and focus on gratitude was a great reminder of how to be human and in Dan's case, a very good one. His message of hard work, discipline and grace made me evaluate my own life and con-sider what it means to be a man. His openness and positivity will help others embrace their vulnerability and that's a gift. And make no mistake, he ain't no mimbo—Dan's the real deal and this is an absolute must read!*"

—Jonas Elrod, writer/director of Wake Up —In Deep
Shift—Conscious Animal

DAN CORTESE

STEP OFF!

MY JOURNEY FROM 'MIMBO' TO MANHOOD

WILEY

Copyright © 2020 by John Wiley & Sons, Inc. All rights reserved.

Published by John Wiley & Sons, Inc., Hoboken, New Jersey.

Published simultaneously in Canada.

No part of this publication may be reproduced, stored in a retrieval system, or transmitted in any form or by any means, electronic, mechanical, photocopying, recording, scanning, or otherwise, except as permitted under Section 107 or 108 of the 1976 United States Copyright Act, without either the prior written permission of the Publisher, or authorization through payment of the appropriate per-copy fee to the Copyright Clearance Center, Inc., 222 Rosewood Drive, Danvers, MA 01923, (978) 750-8400, fax (978) 646-8600, or on the Web at www.copyright.com. Requests to the Publisher for permission should be addressed to the Permissions Department, John Wiley & Sons, Inc., 111 River Street, Hoboken, NJ 07030, (201) 748-6011, fax (201) 748-6008, or online at http://www.wiley.com/go/permissions.

Limit of Liability/Disclaimer of Warranty: While the publisher and author have used their best efforts in preparing this book, they make no representations or warranties with respect to the accuracy or completeness of the contents of this book and specifically disclaim any implied warranties of merchantability or fitness for a particular purpose. No warranty may be created or extended by sales representatives or written sales materials. The advice and strategies contained herein may not be suitable for your situation. You should consult with a professional where appropriate. Neither the publisher nor author shall be liable for any loss of profit or any other commercial damages, including but not limited to special, incidental, consequential, or other damages.

For general information on our other products and services or for technical support, please contact our Customer Care Department within the United States at (800) 762-2974, outside the United States at (317) 572-3993 or fax (317) 572-4002.

Wiley publishes in a variety of print and electronic formats and by print-on-demand. Some material included with standard print versions of this book may not be included in e-books or in print-on-demand. If this book refers to media such as a CD or DVD that is not included in the version you purchased, you may download this material at http://booksupport.wiley.com. For more information about Wiley products, visit www.wiley.com.

Library of Congress Cataloging-in-Publication Data

Names: Cortese, Dan, 1967- author.
Title: Step off! : my journey from mimbo to manhood / Dan Cortese.
Description: First edition. | Hoboken : Wiley, 2020. | Includes index.
Identifiers: LCCN 2020004338 (print) | LCCN 2020004339 (ebook) | ISBN
    9781119653479 (cloth) | ISBN 9781119653462 (adobe pdf) | ISBN
    9781119653486 (epub)
Subjects: LCSH: Cortese, Dan, 1967- | Actors—United States—Biography.
Classification: LCC PN2287.C6315 A3 2020 (print) | LCC PN2287.C6315 (ebook) | DDC
    792.02/8092 [B]—dc23
LC record available at https://lccn.loc.gov/2020004338
LC ebook record available at https://lccn.loc.gov/2020004339

COVER IMAGE: COURTESY OF ENDEAVOR
COVER DESIGN: PAUL McCARTHY

Printed in the United States of America

V10018294_050520

This book is dedicated to my children, Roman, India, and Enzo. You are the lights that ignite my soul and the love that fills my heart. I am blessed and honored to be your father.

CONTENTS

INTRODUCTION

(January 6, 1994—9:00 p.m.) An episode of the sitcom *Seinfeld* titled "The Stall" aired on NBC's Thursday night, "Must See TV" lineup. Like so many people, it was my favorite show on television at the time, and I was making my sitcom debut on this particular episode. I was portraying Elaine's somewhat-vapid, thrill-seeking boyfriend, Tony, who was armed with a catch-phrase symbolic of the 1990s. *"Step off!"* Was I excited? As I was taught to say at the University of North Carolina, "You're darn tootin', fig newton!"—which I believe means, yes. As far as television "street cred" went in the 90s, there was none better than appearing on *Seinfeld*. Obviously, there was no social media at the time, so if you wanted to get yourself "out there" and recognized as a comedic actor, this was the transcendent show to do it on.

Somewhere around the 6:41 mark in the program, a new word was introduced into pop culture folklore. Jerry and Elaine were sitting in his car discussing the reason she was dating Tony. Jerry was adamant it was only for his looks, then he uttered the line, "Elaine, he's a male bimbo...he's a mimbo." The line got a huge laugh and rightfully so, but little did I know, that word spoken on that night would change my life forever.

The following morning, I was leaving a doctor's office in Beverly Hills, where I'd just finished getting a "cast physical" for a new CBS series that I was set to star in with one of my idols, the legendary George C. Scott. I put "cast physical" in quotes because the only thing physical about it was the handshake that doctor who-once-played-a-pimp-on-an-episode-of-Kojak gave me before signing off on my medical well-being. After he filled out all of my paperwork, he felt the need to drop another nugget from his "Tinsel Town" resume, when he dove into some salacious Playboy Mansion–ike details about being Bachelor #2 on *The Dating Game*. I chose that as the perfect time to politely excuse myself. "Have fun with George C., I hear he's a goddamn piece of work," he said, to which I replied, "And you have fun with the pimping; I hear it ain't easy." The echoes of him laughing and spewing on about the research he'd done for the role filled the waiting room like a fart in a Prius.

I left the building, and as I approached my car outside the offices I heard someone yell, "Hey mimbo, step off!" I turned to see a middle-aged white guy whose name I would have bet $100 was Khaki McDockers. It wasn't; good thing I didn't bet. He quickly approached me and giddily shrieked, "Oh my God, it is you. The mimbo!" It was at that moment I realized that, thanks to the power of network television and the comedic brilliance of Jerry Seinfeld, the original mimbo was born . . . me.

Cut to 25 years later, now at the ripe mimbo-fied age of 52, I sit with my iPhone in hand, stressing over which one of two photos would be the more appropriate #TBT post, when I received an email. I wisely chose a baby pic to minimize the troll traffic, then proceeded to check the email. I was happily surprised to see it was from my friend and Instagram bud, Matt Holt, aka senior vice president and executive publisher for Wiley Publishing. This wasn't the typical type of email I'd get from Matt; this one was rather concise and to the point. He'd seen via social media that my third child had just been born and it gave him an idea, so he decided to cast a line. "Have you ever thought about writing a book? Something fun. Something a little more positive than what's out there and a lot more Dan."

Truthfully, over the years the thought had crossed my mind, but that was about it. However, this made things a bit more real, and given the fact that this was someone I truly respected in the publishing world bringing the idea to me, as opposed to the other way around, I felt I'd be doing myself a disservice if I didn't seriously consider it. After going back and forth for a few weeks about the concept, direction, and all the dynamics that go into this process, I was still on the fence. Matt kept coming back to the idea of "a book about Dan." I kept thinking, "A book about Dan. What does he mean by that? I am Dan, and quite frankly, even I'm confused by it." So, I politely said, "We've spoken quite a few times over the years, but have never met face to face. Be perfectly honest with me, because I'm curious. What do you think I'm like as a person?" It was a legitimate question, and I thought his response might help me better understand his vision. He proceeded to tell me that after asking around and speaking with some colleagues, he thought that I would be "a lot like the character I played on that episode of *Seinfeld*, a fun guy who's fun to be around, someone who likes to hang out and have a good time." Unfortunately, through all of his compliments, all I heard was, "You're a male bimbo, you're a mimbo." I wasn't insulted by what he thought I might be like, but I knew I wasn't that character. I knew there was so much more to me than that . . . or was there?

About a week later, Matt introduced me, via email, to bestselling author, speaker, and positivity guru Jon Gordon. If you haven't read any of his books, do so. You can thank me later. After many unnecessary, kind words, he let Jon know, "If you want to know more about Dan, just Google him." Which I decided to do. That's right, I Googled myself, just like every narcissistic actor in Hollywood does on a weekly basis. I wanted to see what Jon would find out about who Dan "really is." In .39 seconds

Google proudly displayed that I'm "Tony the mimbo, from *Seinfeld*," "Jake's brother on Melrose Place," "The Whopper Guy," and apparently "Stefon on SNL mentions Dan Cortese and Twitter goes wild."

Now, while I am truly proud of all of those moments in my life, they more or less define what I've done, not who I am. But the more I thought about it, I realized that how I perceive myself, how I think others perceive me, and how others actually do perceive me, are more than likely, three entirely separate views. So, after speaking with my family, it was with a rather clear realization that I told my friend Matt, "Yes, I'll write the book." I came to the conclusion that if I'm not happy with the narrative of my own story, then maybe I should become the narrator.

If I truly want to do this right, then I'm going to need some honest introspection. So I've put together a collection of life experiences, told as how my brain has chosen to recollect them. As life rapidly passes us by, too often we take the tiny pieces, those little moments, and discard them to the side as if they were irrelevant and unnecessary. This book is a chance for me to do something that all of us should do at some point on our journeys—sit down with open, honest eyes and lay out all of the puzzle pieces of our life on the table. Once you've put them back together, does that finished puzzle look like what you thought it would, or does it look entirely different? Just like any of us who have lived a full life, that's what I'm anxious to find out.

This exploration is an attempt for me to figure out who I really am, and in doing so, will hopefully inspire others to take the time to put their puzzle pieces back together as well. Foundation, Fame, and Fatherhood, this is my journey from mimbo to manhood. At least, that's what I'm hoping takes place, because a journey from mimbo to older mimbo would be pretty damn depressing.

PART 1
FOUNDATION

"WELL... HOW DID I GET HERE?"

"Where we've been is just as important as where we want to go."

Looking back at my life thus far, I have a rather simplistic view of myself. I'm just an average guy who always tried to do what was right and along the way was fortunate enough to live out a dream. But even now, with every new day that dawns, I'm trying to the best of my abilities to navigate this journey for myself and my family. As everyone knows, deep down inside, this shit ain't easy. If you look at people's Instagram pages, though, apparently it's a damn piece of cake. The problem is, I don't eat cake, and (as I think most of us are), I'm just trying to figure it all out as I go along. That being said, here's a brief peek at a few verbal polaroids from my childhood to help you, and me, better understand the Dan that sits here today writing this book.

Meet the Parents

You can't achieve too much success in life without some type of positive foundation. Therefore, meet my positive foundation, my parents Vince and Mary Lou, college sweethearts who have now been happily married for 63 years and are still going strong (Figure 1.1). They've always shown love and respect for each other. Even to this day, any time the song "Heaven Must Be

FIGURE 1.1 My parents, the real MVPs!

Missing an Angel" by Tavaras comes on, they will bust some sick, impromptu dance moves. Not sure why, but my brain loves the random memory of them going all *Dancing with the Stars* in our living room to that jam.

Growing up, my parents were my everything. They were fun, fair, very loving people who always put the kids first and eternally had our backs in the most *Godfather*-like of ways. Both of them worked multiple jobs and constantly busted their asses to provide as best they could for all of us . . . and they still do.

Looking back at it now, even when we went without, we never felt as though we did. If you think about it, making the worst of times feel like the best of times is a pretty damn amazing quality to have as a parent. It's one that I strive to achieve anytime it's necessary to do so with my own children.

My mother is the sweetest, yet strongest, woman you could ever meet. She's always donning a smile on her face and a twinkle in her eye. A cancer survivor with a kind, caring soul who has always been deeply involved with the church. She's not only an incredibly talented seamstress but for years she taught at a school for disabled and special needs children. If there was ever anything we needed, even if it was just a shoulder to cry on, she was there. Her love and support for all of us was the glue that kept our family together.

My father is an Italian immigrant who came to America at the age of six. He was the youngest of seven children and learned how to speak English by being thrust into school a few days after he arrived in the states. Growing up, he diligently went to school during the day, then to work afterward with his father, who was a property caretaker for a few of the wealthier families in town. Because of this, he was forced to accept adult-like responsibilities at a rather young age. But even with all of that on his plate, he persevered and still managed to become the only person in his family to go to and graduate from college. He was our rock, and his love and strength were the foundation that our family was built upon.

House Party

I was the youngest of four children, three boys and one girl, a 10-year difference between myself and my oldest brother, Jim. I wouldn't say I was a "mistake," but I treated my parents to a vacation in Italy a few years ago and after a couple glasses of 1989 Brunello truth serum, my dad admitted to me with a laugh, "I had no idea where the hell you came from!" Check, please!

Needless to say, there was never a dull moment at Casa Cortese, and if any of the boys stepped out of line, my sister, Dianne, was always there to kick any or all of our asses back in it, if need be. A beautiful, caring girl with a heart of gold who never took shit from anyone. For real, if you don't believe me, just ask our neighbor, Chuckie C. who ended up face down in the sewer after bullying her while she was walking home from middle school.

We all grew up in a small suburb, twenty minutes west of downtown Pittsburgh, Pennsylvania, and had an extremely loving, humble home. By "humble," I mean, six people, one bathroom, well-water humble. To be clear, it wasn't like a *Little House on the Prairie* well. I didn't wear a bonnet and walk through fields of barley with a wooden bucket fetching water for Ma and Pa. Okay . . . actually, it was kind of like that, but I was wearing a bandanna instead of a bonnet. Been keeping it real since day one. I only bring all of this up to convey that we were an extremely tight knit family—tighter knit than a *Jersey Shore* Spring Break wardrobe. (Sorry, but for every semi-Italian reference I make, I get a free slice from Mike's Place.)

Boys in My Hood

It's been said, probably by me, that 50 percent of an individual's personality is genetic and the other 50 percent is created by their environment and the people who surround them. To be clear, I don't consider the people I grew up around to be "salt of the earth" types—they're more along the lines of "hot pepper of the earth" types. If you have them in moderation, they're the perfect accompaniment to add a little spice to any and all situations. Too much of them, or if you cross them, and they'll light up your ass. Believe me when I say, these people are the best people I've ever been around, and I wouldn't trade them for anything or anyone. Having lived in Los Angeles for the last 30 years I've come to appreciate just how real the people of Pittsburgh and all of western Pennsylvania are. They don't just have your back—they've got your front, too.

Snapshot, early Summer evening 1979 in Leetsdale, Pennsylvania. Not only was it hot, it was humid AF, as the kids say. The combined odors of pollution, popcorn, Marlboros, and cotton candy fool your brain into believing that this is what fresh air actually smells like. The seats are full, lights are on, and the Quaker Valley Little League All-Star game is in full effect.

The field is located right along the Ohio River Boulevard, a highway that was western Pennsylvania's version of the Autobahn. Just imagine a live version of Mario Kart, only with Buick Electras and AMC Pacers pieced together with duct tape and painted-over putty bumpers hauling ass everywhere. Next to the highway were the train tracks, next to the train tracks was the Ohio River and the only fish you saw in there in 1979 were floating on the top. Across the river were massive billowing smokestacks from a seven-mile stretch of steel mills. I'm sure the sunset was beautiful. It just wasn't usually powerful enough to pierce through the smoke, but on the rare occasion that it did, it gave the field an incredibly cool and probably toxic Studio 54 vibe, so yeah . . . just like Studio 54.

Parents at that time weren't like today's parents. They didn't try to outdo each other by explaining how their kid had a trainer and a nutritionist and was "going pro." (Note to today's parents, 99.99 percent of your kids aren't going pro, so spend more time teaching them to be kind to people.) These parents actually got along, had fun, laughed, cheered, smoked, drank, ate fattening food, and enjoyed the moments together as a community—and all this was just at one Little League game. You should see a Steelers Sunday!

Cut to the final inning of the game, runners on second and third, two outs, we're down 11-10. A 12-year-old, bucktoothed me stepped out of the graffiti-covered dugout and headed toward the batter's box. This was going to be my Rock n' Jock foreshadowing moment, I was going to jack a three-run homer, win the game for us, and walk off with the MVP trophy. In my mind, the cheering crowd of 200 felt more like 20,000. As I stepped into the batter's box, I heard a noise that sounded like what I'd imagine a dolphin would make during a prostate exam. It was our third-base coach, Doc, screaming, "Danny! Danny!" He was flailing his arms so hard there was a good chance he might take flight.

A few things you should know about Doc: He was a lovable guy, the town's OB-GYN, he was accident prone, built like a Weeble, and just hearing his Mr. Bill–like high-pitched voice brought a smile to your face. And—oh yeah—his almost-empty 7Up can was completely full of gin just two innings ago AND he knew absolutely nothing about baseball.

When he saw me looking his way, he screamed, "BUNT!" Parents started to laugh. So did the umpire, so did Doc. He never used signals for the batters, reasoning, "I can't remember the goddamn things." So he giggled, shrugged, and yelled again, "Seriously, bunt it!" I called a timeout and jogged down to him, and he put his arm around me. I swear I caught a respectable frat party–like buzz from his hush-toned breath.

Doc: "I want you to bunt the ball."
 Me: "What?"
Doc: "Yep, bunt the peloto."
 Me: "Peloto?"
Doc: "I think it's Spanish, I'm not sure, I know it's not Chinese. Just bunt it . . . like a bundt cake. No one will ever expect it. Plus, I *really* have to pee."

He slapped my helmet, sent me off, and yelled, "I say B you say unt. B-unt. B-unt!" over and over. The crowd was loving Doc's antics, and as I stepped back into the batter's box, the infielders moved back, thinking it was a ploy. The pitcher went into his wind up and threw a delicious high fastball just like I liked them. I was about to knock the cover off of the ball, but then something happened that I didn't expect to happen. I bunted the freakin' ball! Don't ask me why, but it dribbled down the first base line so slowly, a 90-year-old man taking a piss would've even glanced and smirked. Our runner on third started streaking toward home (not a 1970s kind of streaking, he was just running really fast). I vaguely remember the cheers from the crowd being oddly split between "Go!" and "Are you fucking kidding me!" The pitcher barehanded the ball, threw it home, it sailed over the catcher's head, hit a pole on the backstop and ricocheted like a bullet out near second base. As I got to first base, our second runner, whose name I can't remember, but I do know he was Polish, slid across home plate. Game over, we win, pandemonium ensues! I looked toward third base and Doc was nowhere to be found. Apparently, his two-way pager was blowing up the entire final inning and he had to go deliver twins. As an ironic side note . . . I won the damn MVP (Figure 1.2).

FIGURE 1.2   Not sure why I had my jersey unzipped; maybe I was channeling my inner Tom Jones.

"'JOB' ISN'T JUST A BOOK IN THE BIBLE"
— NO ONE

As an adult, there's one thing that I'm definitely thankful for from my childhood—it's the fact that my parents instilled their work ethic in myself and my siblings. I had many jobs growing up, but here's a snapshot of a few that made the cut and laid a few more bricks onto the foundation of my life.

It was a Saturday in June 1980. A 12-year-old me and my brother Chip were watching one of our favorite shows, *Soul Train*. We watched religiously, specifically to learn any and all new dance moves every week and to get wardrobe ideas. That particular day, right after The Bar Kays crushed a sick, lip-synced performance of "Move Your Boogie Body" laced with ample amounts of red satin and relaxer (YouTube it; you'll thank me later) a commercial came on that changed my life.

A life-sized boombox filled the frame, the massive cassette door on the front of it opened, colored disco lights and smoke filled the air, and out came one of my favorite bands of all time, Earth, Wind & Fire. Sporting more sequins, yet less relaxer than The Bar Kays, their "A" game was on full display. Not only did they dance in unison, singing "Listen to the Power of Platinum," but each member of the group had a Panasonic Platinum boombox on their shoulders. As if it couldn't get any better, they cut to a kid who looked like he could have been the bastard offspring of me and Ralph Macchio. The kid yelled, "Wow! Earth, Wind & Fire!" I took this as a sign from the *Soul Train* gods that I needed the power of platinum in my life. I was given another sign when my father just happened to walk by on his way outside. I had to say something to him.

Me: "Dad, check this out!"
Dad: "That looks pretty cool."
Me: "I know, right? I want that!"
Dad: "You seriously want that?"
Me: "Yes, sir."
Dad: "Okay. Get a job."

And with that, my dad was outside.

I currently had a job mowing Dr. Gayley's lawn, but that type of income wasn't going to cut it, pun intended, if I was going to go platinum. Plus, the fact that the week prior, the doctor asked me why I mowed his lawn twice in four days and reset the mower to its highest cut setting. This led me to believe that I wasn't long for that job.

The next morning, I was on a mission. I got on my Huffy 3 speed with its ballin' black and yellow banana seat and headed 2.2 miles to the Sewickley Heights Golf Club, a beautiful, private club for the preppy, wealthy "Chads" in town, as well as a few Steeler players. My older brothers were caddies there, but I was still a little too young to carry doubles (two bags) for 18 holes. By "too young," I mean scrawny, but in talking with the Caddie Master I found out they needed help in the locker room. This led to me landing a j-o-b that day making the world a brighter place by shining shoes.

Here's the sweet deal I negotiated for myself. I wanted my own office and I got it, i.e., the closet where they kept all of the shoe polish. The rusted AM/FM transistor radio in there was an added bonus that I didn't see coming, but was proof that this was a real damn job. My salary, zero, just the tips. You're welcome.

If a golfer wanted his shoes polished, he'd leave them in front of his locker before he went out to play. Once they were headed to the first hole, I'd run around like Gollum from *The Hobbit* collecting my precious shoes. Then I'd lump them in a massive loafer pile in my office, I remember thinking at one point, "Thom McAn must be ballin.'" With no time to waste, other than to have random thoughts of Thom McAn's bank account, I'd tune the transistor to my favorite station, WAMO, hoping to hear a little "Burn Rubber" by The Gap Band, then I'd commence to polishing my ass off. The gig was basically this: if I did a good job, the golfers would hopefully tip me when they finished their round of golf. I will say, my shining skills were not bad, but if there was one thing I did better, it was talk and kiss ass for that coin. Eddie Haskell had nothing on me.

So, thanks to that skill and the two extra lawn-mowing jobs I picked up, I was listening to the power of platinum by the end of summer.

Be the Ball

From there I was off and running, a lean, mean working machine. By the following summer, I had bulked up a bit and made enough connections to get daily caddying jobs. I even had a few "regulars," which was a golfer who you'd exclusively caddie for when he showed up. I was like a high-end prostitute who had "regular johns," except I carried their bags and cleaned their clubs and balls, so yeah, basically the same thing. I carried doubles for 18 holes, $20 per bag. But again, it was about making those extra tips, so I knew I had to work it.

Two of my regulars were Italian brothers who owned parking structures in downtown Pittsburgh. They were like twin Joe Pesci's from *Goodfellas*, except shorter. These guys were the perfect example as to why stereotypes exist. They oozed profanity, booze, cash, and gold jewelry, and they loved to gamble on their golf matches. One thing they were really good at doing was taking care of their employees. Unfortunately, the one thing they weren't that good at was playing golf.

On specific holes where you couldn't see the fairway from the tee, I'd forecaddie for them. Which means before they'd tee off, I'd haul ass halfway up the fairway to let them know if their ball landed in play after they hit it. So, we had an unspoken agreement that on those specific holes, when their drives would sail out of bounds, I would use whatever means necessary to make sure their shots miraculously landed back in the fairway. I would then be rewarded at the end of the round with a pony bottle of Miller Genuine Draft, a promise that if I ever needed a favor they'd make it happen, and a wad of bills shoved into my hand that made me feel like a young Thom McAn. That being said, I've intentionally left their names out of this recollection, due to the fact that last year they went to prison for doing things other than owning parking structures. Unfortunately, I wasn't around to kick that one back into play for them.

I Don't Give a Tux

Like every kid, I liked money, but even more so, I liked working, and I still do to this day. As I got older, I continued to work as much as possible, but when winter hit in the 'Burgh, the caddying gigs came to a rather abrupt, frostbitten halt.

One winter around the age of 16, I got a job working at a tuxedo rental shop in Ambridge. It was a small town named after American Bridge Steel, which had fallen on extremely hard times after the mills closed down and the steel jobs disappeared. No need to go too deep into detail on this gig, but let's just say that when "wedding and prom season" hit, I wasn't too down with having to measure the inseams of douchey groomsmen with mullets. Plus, they all had the same damn joke, "Is that measuring tape gonna to be long enough?" They'd laugh, high-five their buddies, then mumble dumb shit through their giggles. Imagine a worse version of *Night at the Roxbury*—yeah I said worse, that's what it was like.

I was proud of myself, though; I never made a comment back. I cashed my below-minimum-wage paycheck, and I always intentionally measured their pants an inch and a half short. Looks like it wasn't long enough after all, Sport.

Paint, Sweat, and Beers

As you can probably surmise, I was at a point in my life that when any job would present itself, I'd take it. I was already on my second Panasonic Platinum and also hooked myself up with an affordable (i.e., jenk) version of a Walkman. I think it was called a Groov-E player, not sure. It really didn't matter to me—as long as I could still bump "My Sugar Walls" by Sheena Easton, I was good to go!

As a day job that summer, I was one of four guys hired to help paint houses around town. My experience in this field was zero, unless of course you consider when I was 11 and painted "boobs" on the bottom of my brother's skateboard. To this day he still has no idea it was there...which pretty much defeated the purpose of me painting it. What's not lost is the fact that even to this day it's hilarious to me.

Anyway, I don't think my lack of painting prowess mattered to my boss, since he only paid all of us $5 an hour. But he kept our morale up by buying us the occasional case of Iron City beer after work. It was the perfect way to unwind after eight hours of inhaling paint fumes and would have been a great beer commercial except for the fact that we were 16.

The Fast and Boisterous

During those summer nights, I started working as a valet car parker at the same country club where I had shined shoes and caddied. It seemed like the club would have parties every other night and the rich folks would roll up in their best Brooks Brothers seersucker suits and indulge in an evening of food, fun, and drinks. These soirées gave off vibes of what I thought a semi-classy frat party would be like (if that's even possible). The people that showed up refused to describe the parties as "loud" but, rather, referred to them as "boisterous." Truthfully, I really didn't care what they called them. All I know is that the more boisterous they got, the more they tipped.

This was also where I taught myself how to drive a car with a manual transmission, i.e., "a stick." Once everyone was inside and the party was in full boisterousness, I'd pick a Porsche and turn the parking lot into the Indy 500. By the way, big shoutout to NFL Hall of Famer and Pittsburgh Steeler legend, Lynn Swann, for, unbeknownst to him, letting me utilize his car to get my inner Mario Andretti on.

I met him years later in 1994. We were two of the competitors in Major League Baseball's All-Star Celebrity Homerun Derby. While I didn't tell him about driving his car, I felt the need to let him know that I was the valet who, at every party, would change all of the stations on his car radio to WAMO. It felt good to clean that from my conscience and even better to think that maybe, just maybe, thanks to me, he was introduced to the sweet sounds of Vanity 6. To this day I still envision Lynn driving to Steeler practice singing "Nasty Girl" to himself.

The Heat Is On . . . Painted On

At one point I also worked in downtown Pittsburgh at PPG Place. It was a gorgeous all-mirrored high-rise complex centered in the heart of the city. The only problem was, if you didn't know exactly where you were going, you'd get lost in there for hours. It was like Bobo's House of Mirrors at the county fair. Only difference was, everyone there was wearing suits and ties and had most of their teeth.

I've got to admit, it was the first time I felt like I had a real job. Although some of that feeling may have had to do with the fact that this was also the first time I had to purchase "slacks and loafers" to wear for work. Just a side note, if you're in your 20s and you use the words "slacks and loafers" and/or wear slacks and loafers, chances are you'll be leaving the bar alone, Potsie. Believe me when I say that; I speak from experience.

Anyway, I worked as an intern at a modeling and casting agency. This place was basically a rung or two above Glamour Shots. I was genuinely excited about the opportunity, because I honestly thought this was something close to working in the entertainment business. Could this be the chance I'd always hoped I'd get?

Two very successful but very loud women owned the company. Trust me they weren't boisterous, they were straight up "loud broads" (their words, not mine). At my interview I was told that their definition of an intern meant that I wouldn't get paid and that they just needed someone to do whatever they were told to do and answer the phones, because, "Gina spread 'em and went and got knocked up . . . AGAIN!" They laughed, so I did too, and buttoned it with an "Ohhhh, that Gina." After a long, awkward silence, the one with the red perm told me I was "kinda cute" and that I should go ahead and start immediately, which I proceeded to do.

The job was a fun one I guess, much easier than painting houses. Although, on occasion when it was a slow day on the phones, I'd find myself lost in a melancholy daze longing for the times of Benjamin Moore fumes and Iron City beer, free from nut-hugging slacks and loafers. Sadly, this wasn't turning out to be the "big break" I had hoped for—or was it?

On a rainy day, the bosses ordered lunch in and got me some as well; this was a first. They asked me to join them to eat and proceeded to tell me that the company was in contention for a "gig" with the Miami Heat and wanted me to help them out with it. Hell yes, I was all about this! Was I going to fly to Miami? Would I get to meet the team? Would I get to dress in pastels and go all Tony Montana with Crockett and Tubbs? Unfortunately, it stopped just a bit shy of all of that, when out of a Foot Locker bag appeared a Miami Heat t-shirt that would have been snug on a six year old.

Cut to me, so squeezed into the shirt that the president of Hooters was on line two with an offer. They had me standing in front of the office "photo wall." One woman was snapping pics like Herb Ritts on Red Bull, the other was wetting me down with a spray bottle filled with ice water or ice cold vodka, not sure. Actually, given the way they were acting, I'll lean toward the latter. I wondered if this was similar to what Burt Reynolds had to endure for his *Playgirl* spread.

When they were finished, I remember Rosie Permhair saying, "I think this could be your big break, Dan." 2019 Dan wishes he would have responded with a simple, "Me too." Side note . . . there was no Miami Heat gig. Oh well, you live and learn, Champ. At least I got a free lunch out of the deal.

Sleep Cheap

During my senior year of high school I was hired as a weekend maintenance man at a Red Roof Inn hotel. This job stands out in my mind for one major reason, that being, I wasn't the handiest kid on the block. Luckily, the job didn't require me to be proficient in anything too difficult. My job requirements consisted of things like mowing the property grounds, changing light bulbs, touch up painting, and basically helping the staff with whatever they needed. A good majority of the time helping was spent attempting to unclog toilets. Regarding those clogged toilets, I'd like to remind people who stay in hotels that hand towels should ONLY be used to wipe your hands, hence the name.

The company also had a rule that after each guest checked out, the housekeeping staff had to flip the mattresses before changing the sheets for the next guest. Let's just say that after assisting with that on one occasion, I was cool with the clogged toilets. I find it hard to put into words what traveling businessmen chose to put in between the mattresses upon departure from a hotel. Seriously, even as a 17-year-old kid, I was like, "Fellas, it can't be THAT bad at home!" When said items would be exposed, the housekeeping staff thought it was funny to leave them in my office, i.e., the maintenance closet. Because of this, I had a collection of untitled magazines and untouchable novelties that would even make Ron Jeremy go, "Oh wow! That's something I haven't seen before." So, trust me when I tell you, I've seen things.

On a less "ewww" note, one of the perks of the job had to do with my uniform. I was required to wear a t-shirt with the company slogan on it, and that slogan was an all-time winner: "Sleep Cheap." The shirts came in red or white, and I had a big ol' box of them in the maintenance closet. You couldn't purchase them anywhere, they weren't available in any stores—that's right, not even Spencer Gifts or Hot Topix had the access I did.

As a result, selling these to my teenage buddies became a pretty sweet side hustle. You could say, I was basically a high school t-shirt pimp who had no need for a sales pitch. Think about it, in 1986 what teenage boy wouldn't want to divert attention away from his acne-covered face with a sweet "Sleep Cheap" tee? No need to lay a rap down to the ladies when your shirt and smirk said it all for you. I sold only a few at first and labeled them as "limited edition" to help drive up the price. Not positive, but pretty sure this might have been where Ty Warner got the idea to do the same thing with Beanie Babies. I should probably have my attorney look into that. (Note to self: Hire an attorney.)

A few days before I was about to go out with my second round of sales, my P.E. teacher shut down the whole operation because I wouldn't give him one for free. Here's the type of guy my P.E. teacher was. Each side of his car had a different hubcap style. Why? Because he thought people would believe he had a second car if they happen to see it from the other side. Actually, now that I think about it, that's exactly the type of guy that I'd expect would ask a 17-year-old for a free "Sleep Cheap" t-shirt. Unfortunately, with that, my dreams of apparel dominance came to an abrupt inventory-heavy halt. Just for the record, Coach, nobody thought you had two maroon Honda Accords.

SCHOOL DAZE

Even though I basically worked throughout my teens, those jobs meant nothing more to me than necessary money in my pocket. Grade school on through middle and high school had a few distinct and defining moments for where my life was headed and how I would get there.

The truth was, by fifth grade I knew what I wanted to do for a living. I remember our class was chosen to put on a play for the entire school and parents, so what better choice than *Alice in Wonderland*. Actually it was some sort of bizarre mash-up of *Alice* mixed with a few random outspoken time travelers. Apparently, there was no drug testing for the schoolteachers back in the 1980s.

Every student had a role in the play, and I felt mine was a rather pivotal one. No, not The White Rabbit or King of Hearts, or even The Cheshire Cat, I had a role created specifically for me, but not for the reasons one may think. I remember approaching my rather hardass teacher Ms. Wilson and politely asking her for one of the leading roles. Without even looking in my direction, she let me know that there were some "really talented kids who can actually act" in the class and they'd be getting the bigger parts. But since she'd seen me wear a brown vest at the Christmas Show, she thought I'd be perfect to play a new character added to the play called "The Brown Rabbit." The Brown Rabbit had one scene where he brought tea to Alice and The White Rabbit, and if my MTV-fried brain recalls correctly, his one and only line was, "Here's some tea for you." During rehearsals, I crushed that line, delivering it with identical, Brown Rabbit–like stoic monotony every single time.

Then when show night arrived, something happened, not sure how or why, but it just did. A few beats before I was to make my entrance, I was handed a tray of teacups filled with water. Then all I heard was, "Brown Rabbit get out there!" I slowly entered the stage, set the tray down, handed out two cups of tea and delivered my line with ease. After Alice thanked me for the tea, I was supposed to exit the stage, but for some reason, I picked up a cup for myself, downed it, and as I started to walk off stage, I said, "Ahhh, now that's some dang good eatin'." The next moment felt as if it was in slow motion. Off stage, I saw Ms. Wilson's incensed eyes lock onto mine Terminator-style, and I knew I'd be getting the paddle. But then something unexpected occurred. The entire auditorium erupted with laughter and applause. Her glare turned into a semi-approving smirk and she gave me a light backhand slap to my head as I passed by walking off stage.

The feeling I got that day was one that I've remembered my entire life, and it still gives me goosebumps thinking about it. I wanted that feeling. I wanted to do this for a living. I wanted to entertain people. But not just entertain them, I wanted to walk that fine line between getting applause and getting the paddle. Because if there's no chance in either occurring, then what's the point in attempting it? I wholeheartedly felt that this was what I was meant to do.

Seeing Is Believing, But Feeling Is Knowing

A few years later, I had what I would consider to be an enlightening premonition. I know what you're thinking. "Dan, isn't that a bit dramatic? I get that you wanted to be an actor, but bruh, c'mon, an enlightening premonition?" Yes, it's a bit dramatic, but I'm really not sure how else to describe it.

I was in the car with my mother, we were on our way back to Pittsburgh from my sister's house in Ohio. As we rolled down the onramp of exit 234 on the Ohio Turnpike and headed home, I was overcome with a feeling of what I would describe as, warmth and positive affirmation associated with what my life would become. I recall my mother asking why I was so quiet, so I told her about what had occurred. Then, I'm not sure why, but I felt the need to let her know that I was going to be fine and that she wouldn't have to worry about me in the future. I concluded my response by expressing that it was okay for me to follow my dream of being an entertainer, because the premonition let me know that it was what I was meant to do. To which my beautiful mother kindly replied, "If that's what you want to do, then I'm sure you will, sweetie."

As odd as it seems re-reading that, I truly believe with all of my being that something in the Universe communicated with me that day, and I've never doubted it for a second since. As my life sped forward, I always felt that my future had a safety net. I'm not sure if it was someone or something guiding me, but it put my young teenage mind, surprisingly at ease. It sounds silly, it sounds naïve, it might even sound irresponsible and egotistical, but it made sense to a teenager with newfound confidence and helped to build strength and character that would become necessary as I entered high school.

I Lived in the Principal's Office . . . Literally

All of us who've gone to high school, no matter what year or what town, know of the stresses that accompany those awkward years. They're by no means easy times, but they're times when many of us are tested by life to help us discover what type of person we are and what we're made of.

All of that being said, my high school years were just a bit different than the average student, as my journey came with an obstacle that very few have ever experienced. As I alluded to earlier in the book, my father was an extremely hard-working man who always put his family ahead of himself. In wanting the best for all of us, he constantly kept striving for more, so much so that after many years of teaching and coaching, he became a high school principal . . . MY high school principal. Yep, let that sink in and simmer in the third-period study hall of your brain for a sec. Puberty, zits, Peter Brady–like voice cracks, and B.O. all took a back seat to the stress of having my dad as my principal.

I remember the morning of my first day of high school like it was yesterday. I walked into the kitchen for breakfast where my father was waiting for me with a smile on his face that could've graced Hollywood movie posters. He's a good lookin Dego, for sure. The aroma that filled the kitchen was a sweet mixture of freshly brewed coffee and Brut cologne. Actually, reading that, it doesn't sound so sweet, but damn it, he rocked it, and somehow he made it work like a badass. He gave me a hug, then put his Andre the Giant–sized mitts on my shoulders.

Dad: "I love you. First day of high school, are you excited?"
Me: "Yes, sir."
Dad: "Me, too. You look good."
Me: "Thanks, dad."
Dad: "I mean, if that's the way you want to look." (I still use that line on my kids to this day.)

We shared a laugh at that joke I'd heard a hundred times, but it got my mind off of the pressures of the day, albeit briefly. He turned around, swooped a brown-bag lunch off of the kitchen counter, and handed it to me. Dad made my lunch practically every day of high school so that my mom would have one less thing to worry about as she got ready for work. It was always the same thing per my request, two PB&J's, a bag of greasy ass, generic potato chips, and whatever Hostess or Little Debbie snack was on sale at Giant Eagle that week. Looking back, maybe my diet had something to do with my Clearasil poster-boy good looks.

My dad downed the rest of his coffee and headed to the door, then he paused, looked over his shoulder at me, and suddenly turned into Robert De Niro from *Godfather II*.

Dad: "Listen. We don't have any problems at school, then we don't have any problems at home. Capisci?"

I nodded my head in agreement, then he winked at me, smiled, and left. If there was one thing I knew as a teenager, it was the importance of recognizing when my father meant business. Even though he spoke calmly, I knew this was one of those times.

Fortunately, I understood the pressures of his job as well. How could he expect parents to respect him disciplining their kids if he couldn't control his own? The fact that we were both on the same page and understood that we had each other's back strengthened our relationship through those challenging years. Plus, I was driven to succeed to make him and my mother as proud as I possibly could.

Truthfully, it was pretty damn cool to have my father as my principal, whether it was busting my balls as I'd try to talk to a girl at her locker or occasionally having me called out of class to his office just to tell me that he loved me. I wouldn't have wanted it any other way. I was blessed to have both of my parents at every game, every dance, every school event, and I loved it. It created a special bond between us that I attempt to mirror with my own children.

As my high school years came to a close, I was a three-year letterman in two sports, never missed the honor roll, and never had one day of detention. I remember all of those times often and with great fondness. My freshman year at the University of North Carolina and my first-semester 1.8 GPA is another story, but I prefer to end this chapter on a high note, capisci?

CHAPEL THRill

It always amazes me when I look back on specific occurrences in and around my life and absorb how they've affected my journey thus far. Not the obvious ones, but the simple unassuming ones, which, at the time they occurred, might not have seemed very relevant. As time rapidly passes, I've come to realize and appreciate that it's the simple honesty of those unassuming moments that invigorates life and gives it relevance. As with all of us, if certain tiny moments had never occurred along the way, then my story would have gone in a completely different direction. I began to become more keenly aware of this once I started college, possibly because I believed I was starting to make sense out of life. Even if it was very little sense, it was some sense, nonetheless.

What If

As I mentioned at the close of the last chapter, I was fortunate enough to attend college at the University of North Carolina, in lovely Chapel Hill. It was always my favorite college growing up, not because of the stellar academics it's known for, but more so thanks to Michael Jordan and the Tar Heels basketball team. As a high school student I dreamed of going there, but I never believed it could even be an option for me. The reality of it just seemed so unattainable and, as silly as it sounds, so far away. So, the question is, how did some random kid from western Pennsylvania end up in Chapel Hill?

One random Saturday night in the fall of 1985, my oldest brother Jim, aka JC, decided to go out for a few beers with friends. Now you've got to understand, he has just as much fun as anybody when he goes out, but more often than not, JC prefers to stay in. That night he headed to Mike's Place, an Italian restaurant/bar, "locals only" kind of joint in my hometown. It was right near the Ohio River Boulevard and owned by my buddy's dad, whose English was so broken even putting a cast on his tongue wouldn't have helped him. It was the first time JC had ever been there, but once inside he ran into quite a few people he knew, one of them being Phil Zacharias, a friend from high school he hadn't seen in at least 10 years.

Phil was a great guy, a family friend who was laid back and cool as could be. Among other things, Phil asked how our family was and what I was up to. Jim told him I was a senior quarterback for the high school and was pretty sought after by a number of colleges. In my mind, Phil said, "No freaking way?!" but in reality I'm sure his response was much closer to something like, "Cool. Good for Danny." Phil then proceeded to tell Jim that he was working as a graduate assistant football coach at the University of North Carolina and that I should send game film to the UNC coaching staff. Then as simple as that, the conversation changed. If I know JC, it was probably because a good-looking girl walked in, and that was that.

When JC told me the next day about the potential opportunity, I was excited but wasn't sure if anything would ever come of it. But even as a teenager, I believed in the power of positivity, so I sent the coaches a few tapes of my best games and kept my fingers crossed. I'd been busting my ass training so hard for the last three years, maybe this was why. Truthfully, I would have been happy with just a written response on Carolina letterhead. But as luck would have it, badda-bing-badda-boom, one response letter and one visitation trip to Chapel Hill later, I agreed to become a member of the Tar Heels football team.

But once I began my freshman year, the reality and responsibility associated with my college life was a blindside hit I wasn't prepared for. Turns out when you're busy trying to manage a full course load, playing football, being away from home and—thanks to all of it—doing it on very little sleep, chances are you're probably not going to do well in any facet of college life. Hence, the fall semester 1.8 GPA. Truth is, I loved playing football and the comradery that accompanied it, but by the end of my second year of playing for the Tar Heels, I knew something needed to change. Plus, I'd had a few signs—a back injury, a coaching change—that it was time to hang up my cleats. I decided to pay more attention to my grades. It was a decision that wasn't easy to make given the many years of hard work I'd put into the sport, but it was necessary as I headed into a new chapter of my life.

Looking back, I've come to realize that the random meeting between my brother and Phil wasn't about football at all. It was about the universe working it's magic and presenting an opportunity that positively affected the course of my life. I truly believe the reason for all of my training and hard work wasn't to play football but to be capable enough to physically get me where I needed to be at a specific point in time in order to take the next step in my life. My preparation, in essence, was for what was to come afterward.

This proved to be the perfect example for me to always be open, awake, and aware that everything that's happening is happening for a reason. Had I not gotten into Carolina, my backup plan would have taken me on a different path. I more than likely would have ended up becoming a cadet at the Naval Academy that fall. Something tells me that the road from the military to MTV may have been a bit bumpier than the one I took. "What's up, it's Lieutenant Dan Cortese, and this is *MTV Sports!*" . . . now THAT would have been extreme.

Bar(pre)tender

By my junior year, I had college down to a science. Grades were up, football was in the rearview mirror, and now all I needed was some money to subsidize my Domino's doubles addiction. On a Friday afternoon I walked into Four Corner's. It was one of the hottest bars on campus and I was hoping to land a job, any kind of job. I wasn't going to be picky. I was pointed in the direction of an extremely pissed off woman who, I was told, was the manager. She was standing at the end of the bar writing something in a notebook so ferociously that I was pre-planning my counter move in case she came at me. I recall the conversation going as follows:

> **Me:** "Excuse m . . . "
> **Manager:** "What?!"
> **Me:** "Hi, my name is Dan, and I was just stopping by to see if you possibly had any jobs available?"

She slammed her pen down and yelled, "HA!" I was starting to think one counter move wouldn't be sufficient. She glared at me for a long beat, almost as if she knew I was thinking about counter moves.

Manager: "How old are you?"
  Me: "Twenty-one."
Manager: "Do you bartend?"
  Me: "Yes, ma'am."
Manager: "Well then, Dan, this is your lucky day! I just fired a bartender two minutes before you walked in for stealing from us. Will you steal from us, Dan?!"
  Me: "No, ma'am."
Manager: "Good! You start Monday. Be here at five ready to work."

With that, she walked off and I walked out of the bar wondering what the hell just happened. The good news was, I was going to bartend at the best bar in town. The bad news, I didn't have a damn clue how to bartend. On the bright side, I'd seen Tom Cruise in *Cocktail* a few times, so I was feeling pretty good about my chances. That's not a joke, that was my actual thought process at 21.

That weekend I crammed harder on *Sardi's Bar Guide* than any final I'd ever taken up to that point. Not sure what that says about my priorities or academic prowess, but I didn't care. I was going to make this work no matter what. When Monday rolled around, I showed up on time, teeth brushed with my cheesy Tom Cruise smile ready to smirk on cue. Once I finished strategically placing my drink recipe cheat sheets around the bar, I was ready to work. My bartending business guide consisted of these three things:

1. Making frozen drinks takes too much time, therefore you lose out on other tips. So when anyone would order a frozen drink, I'd tell them the blender was broken and offer them a free shot and a beer instead.

2. If I made a drink wrong or if I was told it "didn't taste right" (usually by some condescending jackhole businessman), I would tell them, "Sorry, that's how we make it here. But if you'd like, I can give you a free shot and a beer instead."

3. Always make the first drink strong AF! Nothing better than seeing someone take a sip of their Long Island iced tea, grimace in pain, then say, "Ohhhhh, that's good."

If there was one thing I knew and remembered from my valet parking days, the bigger the buzz, the bigger the tip. Also, I'm sure there are some of you reading this who are questioning my character for giving out free shots and beers. After all, I told the manager that I wouldn't "steal" from the bar. The truth is, I took one business class in college and I remember two things from it. One, always keep the customer happy; therefore, I didn't consider this "stealing," I looked at it more as good "customer service" because they always seemed to be really happy. Two, I got a C– in that class. So, there's your answer . . . would you like a free shot and a beer to go with that?

General College

One rainy Saturday afternoon, my roommate and I decided to step out of the comfort and unidentifiable odor of our 12×13 dorm room and try something that I was very intrigued by. The university funded a student-run "television show" that not only starred students from the school but was written, directed, and produced by them as well. It was a soap opera called *General College*, which aired weekly on the public access station in Chapel Hill, and I was headed to audition for a new role.

It was my first-ever audition, and I was fortunate enough to land the part. I'm not positive why I got the part, but it may have been because I don't recall seeing anyone else there auditioning for it. Either way, I was happily cast as Kyle Donovan, the all-star freshman soccer goalie whose mullet was big and his ego was bigger. That season's story arc saw Kyle allow zero scoring on the field, but do plenty of it off. Unfortunately, one night in an alcohol-induced rant about "chicks and scoring," Kyle plummeted off a sixth-floor dorm balcony, only to wake up and find himself parapalegic.

Thanks to the drunken tumble, Kyle lost his scholarship and was on suicide watch 24/7. His popularity had plummeted and he wanted to end it. But with the help of his nurse, he was able to overcome all of that, by once again scoring . . . with his nurse . . . in his wheelchair. What did you expect? It was a soap opera written by 20-year-olds. Work with me, people.

Surprisingly, the show became successful enough to be picked up by NCTV (National College Television), a small cable network out of New York that aired in over 300 college towns. The truth of the matter is, while I enjoyed every moment of working on *General College*, I always thought the show was really campy. That was, until I worked on *Melrose Place* for nine episodes; then I realized it WAS really campy, but in such a glorious way that it could hold its soap opera–own with the likes of *Melrose* any day. Now that I think about it, how has Netflix not rebooted this yet?

Looking back on it all, I realize this was one of those moments in time where I was being prepared for what my future had in store for me. It was a fantastic boot camp for working

on a real production, no matter how small. It helped me to gain
more confidence in front of the camera without a lot of pressure,
due to the fact that it was produced by my peers. (At this time,
I'd like to thank the good folks at YouTube for not making my
over-the-top, down-the-back-mullet acting readily available via
a quick search.)

REALITY CHECK

The summer before my senior year at UNC, I got a job working at a small steel mill in Wampum, Pennsylvania. It was a little over 40 miles west of downtown Pittsburgh near the Ohio border with a town population just under 800 people. There may not have been a lot of people in town, but trust me, they were the epitome of hard-working, western Pennsylvania folks that the region is so well known for.

I had a meeting with the foreman the day before I started. There I was told that, since I wasn't union, I wouldn't get union wages, since I wasn't a skill worker, I'd be given a specific job each day and the only hours available to work would be the "graveyard shift." Which was appropriately named because the shift hours spanned from midnight to 8 a.m., sometimes noon if anyone called in sick. Then I was told not to call in sick. Truthfully, this was all good with me, because I'd be making $11/hour, which in my college mind was basically equivalent to an NBA contract today.

The first night I showed up for work I was given a locker and a respirator and was pointed to the job board, which was nothing more than a chalkboard with everyone's duties for the night written on it. My name was always at the very bottom and always had the same job next to it, "Utility Man." All this meant was that I'd be given the worst job that no one else wanted. I'll just say, ain't no toilet quite like a steel mill toilet, not even a Red Roof Inn one.

I eventually worked my way up to occasionally "making mixes," mixes of what, to this day I still have no clue. Along with my lead-based gloves and apron, I was told to put on my respirator and under no circumstances take it off when I was making them. I would then be given the mix recipe, which was usually a torn piece of paper with a list of about a dozen chemicals I couldn't pronounce. Each one came in a bag of 50 to 100 pounds and covered with more skulls and crossbones than the Virgina Beach Tattoo Festival when Motley Crüe performed. I would then collect the bags and take them to the baking vat, which was located in a room that was about 120 degrees. Once in there, the steps were, turn on the oven, turn on the vat, dump in the chemicals, turn on the mixer, wait five minutes, then hit a blue button to start the process, wait five minutes, then hit a green button to finalize the process. All while trying not to inhale. Come to think of it, whatever I inhaled in that room was more than likely the cause of my fashion choices from the early to mid-90s.

The first few weeks I stayed pretty much to myself, and by that I mean, no one would talk to me or eat with me. I didn't take it personally because everyone there was twice my age, plus the "graveyard shift" had a different vibe to it, which was hard for a 21-year-old kid like me to understand. These guys were steel mill lifers, real men with real-world problems who had been working the "graveyard" for years. They had wives and kids, but still chose to work the graveyard to make a few extra dollars to take care of their families, as best they could.

One night I was given a crash course in how to drive a forklift, crash being the key word there. Let's just say Dave the foreman wasn't real chipper after I drove the forks through a warehouse garage door. "It's a forklift, Dan, not a what-the-fuck-lift!" Dave was basically the leader of the "lifers" by default, one of those guys that refused to wear his respirator just so he could smoke while he worked. I'll see your cancer causing chemicals and raise you a Camel, no filter.

In some odd way I think the forklift mishap endeared me to Dave and a few of the guys there. Because that night they invited me to join them on meal break. I finally felt like I was one of the crew. I was never in a frat in college and never wanted to be; these Phi Kappa Hard-Asses were as close as I came, and I was appreciative of their welcoming me. I actually still tell myself that I think they might have enjoyed listening to my stories of college parties and bartending ineptitude. They didn't, but I tell myself that.

I remember one night toward the end of the summer, it was pouring outside, we were on a meal break and the mood was different than ever before. The conversation between the crew was subdued, heartfelt, and extremely honest. Maybe it was the rain or maybe there was a full moon hiding behind the clouds. Mikey, my forklift instructor, almost broke down telling a story about how he's worked the graveyard for three years straight so he could afford to build a pool for his kids. But while they now had a pool, they still didn't have a relationship with him because he was always either at the mill or immediately going to sleep once he got home. As I think about it now, the moment had an extreme *Shawshank* vibe to it, so I in turn decided to share my thoughts.

Going into my senior year, with the real world looming just a few months ahead of me, I was starting to question some of my choices. I stopped working on *General College*, I had no connections to the entertainment industry, and even if I did, realistically, what kind of living could I make at it? So I told them something that I hadn't told anyone, that I was thinking about taking some time off from school or maybe even quitting altogether. I used the bogus excuse that I wanted to "reevaluate my life." I remember the three of them just staring at me for the longest beat. The only thing I could hear was the driving rain pounding on the metal roof over our heads.

Mikey looked at me almost as if I'd just told him his dog had died. Then in a very calm tone, he said, "I like you, Cortese, so you might want to listen to me. You're a goddamn idiot. You don't realize the opportunity you've been given. I'm 42 and wish someone would have given one to me. Instead, I'm here and my kids only know me as the guy that bought them a pool."

It made a little sense to me then, but not as much as it makes now. When you're young and naïve, sometimes you need to hear things in a way that you can relate to, and that's exactly what happened next. As the three of them sat in silence, seemingly lost in thoughts of what might have been, Mikey lit up a smoke, took a long contemplative drag off of it, and very simply said something that changed my life forever.

"Look, it's your life, so do whatever you want to. But I promise you this, if we see you working here next summer and you tell us you dropped out of college, we will beat the living shit outta you." He stared a hole through me for a good three seconds after that, then leaned his head back, took another drag, and closed his eyes.

Needless to say, I made the right decision, and after that summer I never saw any of them again. But believe me when I say, I think of that meal break every day and I'm continually amazed how a seemingly simple, unassuming moment became such a pivotal one in my life. Maybe it was the rain, maybe it was a full moon hidden behind the clouds, or maybe it was me getting hit with an uppercut of common sense. Yep, sometimes you just need to hear things in a way that makes sense to you.

MS. JACKSON if YOU'RE NASTY

March 2, 1990, three months shy of my UNC graduation date, I found myself in the RTVMP (radio, television, and motion picture) building sitting in a professor's office complaining about a grade for a media project I had handed in. His name not only escapes me now but always did when I was taking his course. Thanks to his uncanny appearance, I only ever referred to him as "Richard Dreyfuss" and, on occasion, "Beard Dandruff." Therefore, for the sake of this memory, he will remain "Richard Dreyfuss." Anyway, I didn't necessarily think my project was better than the grade I was given, but it was rumored that Richard

Dreyfuss could be persuaded into a grade change if a student made an impassioned plea.

So, there I was in his office dripping melodrama. This moment was proof that scheduling my classes for two years around watching the acting on *Days of Our Lives* was a good idea. I finished my appeal to him with a distorted facial expression caught somewhere between a lip quiver and "the white man's overbite." Yes, it was an awkward unrehearsed look, but I was in too deep not to commit to it. With that, Richard Dreyfuss looked down and silently opened his grade book, slowly tapped his Bic on the desk, then after a long beat and deep breath he looked up and said...nothing. In perfect Richard Dreyfuss dramatic fashion, right as he was about to speak, his phone rang. As he reached for the phone with one hand, he held up the index finger of the other, and damn it if his fingernail didn't steal the scene. I remember thinking, either he plays the flamenco guitar or Richard Dreyfuss is secretly Dracula. I was so taken aback by the nail that all I really remember of his phone conversation were a few "Yes's", "sure's," and an "of course."

He finished the call, hung up the phone, closed his grade-book, and leaned back in his creaky professor chair. Then he said, "Young man,"—he probably called me young man because he didn't know my name, either. Maybe he called me "Chachi" when talking to the rest of his flamenco band—"Young man, I'm not going to change your grade, but I've got an offer for you. On the phone was a producer from MTV. Janet Jackson is in concert on campus tomorrow night and they're shooting a live special from it. They need a few gophers for the shoot—40 bucks cash, and you can put it on your resume." Instantly, his nail didn't seem so creepy and I gladly accepted his offer with a confirming handshake. Truth is, I wanted my MTV a helluva lot more than I wanted that grade bump. While I thought my recorded audio dissection of the Parliament Funkadelic song "Knee Deep" deserved an A, I'm sure Richard Dreyfuss only understood a C+ worth of the material, so I was good with it.

The next day couldn't get there quick enough. I mean, let's be honest, it was 1990 and there was ABSOLUTELY NOTH-ING cooler than MTV. I showed up early for work wearing a Carolina T-shirt and my ripped jeans, which I had strategically tucked into my hightop Nikes—yeah, I had it like that. The pro-ducer in charge of the shoot, Robert LaForty, quickly made me swap out the Carolina tee for an MTV one, which I happily threw on over top. The first thing that went through my mind was that if he asked for the shirt back at the end of the night, I knew I could totally outrun him. He surprisingly made no comment about the jeans tucked into my hightops, but then again, he also had curly, long red locks that would have made Kip Winger jealous, so he was probably down with the look.

The talent on the shoot was none other than Downtown Julie "Wubba, wubba, wubba" Brown. LaForty took note of my massive size, or lack thereof, and gave me my marching orders for the night. For some reason I was assigned to be Julie's body-guard for the live shoot. We were going to be filming amongst the commoners and he chose all 6 foot, 170 pounds (on a good day) of me to keep the masses away from DTJB. I looked at this as a golden opportunity, not to get to know Julie or even to prove myself to the good people of MTV, but to get my damn face on television. Every time we went live, I made it a point to seek out someone near her and make them give Julie "some space," then I would stand there "holding people back" with my arms out-stretched and flexing so hard that I was bursting blood vessels in my eyes. I didn't care, I was willing to do whatever it took to get on camera, even if it meant fighting through partial blindness and crippling muscle cramps to do so.

In the midst of the shoot, I realized I was not only having a great time, but that this could potentially turn into an amazing opportunity for me. I mean c'mon, this was MTV! So, I was dead set on busting my ass to do the best job I possibly could. After the concert was over, I got paid my 40 bucks and was surprisingly invited back to the crew hotel for drinks with everyone. Forty dollars, an MTV t-shirt, AND beer? Pretty sure this was going on my greatest-night-ever list.

After wandering around the hotel for 15 minutes thinking I was punked, I found the MTV suite where everyone was hanging out. I was quickly greeted with the bad news—the crew wanted brew and Julie needed champagne. One problem, this was Chapel Hill, not New York City, it was past 1 a.m., the bars were closed, and room service refused to serve alcohol. I remember everyone figuring we'd have to call it a night, but I wanted my MTV and my B-E-E-R, so I said, "Let me see what I can do," and exited the room with the confidence of David Hasselhoff in a Speedo. The truth of the matter was, I had no fucking clue what I was going to do, but I went into Old School Pittsburgh Baller mode and headed to the lobby. There was one guy working the front desk, and if I didn't know better, I would have thought it was Cooter from the *Dukes of Hazzard*. Hell, it was North Carolina, it might have actually been Cooter.

I briefly explained our dire situation. We needed two bottles of champagne and a 12-pack of beer. Then I dropped the names Downtown Julie Brown and MTV so many times that my squat max increased by 200 pounds just picking them back up. Cooter just looked at me with the dead eyes of someone working the Embassy Suites graveyard shift. I knew there was only one solution if dropping names alone didn't work.

I had recently applied for and received a student AMEX card. Not only hadn't I used it, I hadn't even signed the back yet. I slid it on the check-in desk like someone who could actually pay the monthly bill (perception is 99% of the game). Next to the AMEX, I threw the two crisp twenties I had just received for working the night and said, "The AMEX is for the drinks, the cash is for you, and so is this." In one fluid motion, I took off my MTV shirt, folded it, and set it down next to the cash. Thankfully, I still had on my Carolina shirt underneath or else the story would have taken an odd turn. Cooter looked at the shirt and his eyes lit up almost as if Daisy Duke had just invited him into the woodshed.

Next thing you know, the door to the MTV suite swung open (cue the slow-motion effect and wind machine) and there stood Dan-o, a 12 pack of Busch Beer in one hand and two bottles of champagne in the other. It took me six months to pay it off on my AMEX, plus late fees. But I didn't care. I got my MTV, I got my beer, and I got LaForty's business card, with an "If you're ever in New York and are looking for work…" promise attached to it.

On that day I experienced something that I would later come to realize many times over—something that only a select few who have worked at the network know. In the 1990s, there was almost nothing more powerful than the MTV t-shirt. Trust me, an entire book could be written on that topic alone.

GO BIG OR GO HOME

With the excitement of the "MTV connection" still fresh in my mind, I decided to go all in on a plan that, up until that point, I'd been about 50/50 on. My father used to have a saying about delaying making a much-needed decision. He'd say, "Either shit or get off the pot." At 22 years of age I chose to make a decision that would change my life forever. I decided it was "go time" and time for me to get going.

I was 100 percent in on pursuing my acting dreams, but in being honest with myself, I knew my best chances wouldn't be waiting for me in Pittsbugh or Chapel Hill. In my mind, there was only one way to do it, and that was to move to Los Angeles immediately after graduation. Go big or go home! As exhilarating and powerful as it was to commit to this, I'd be lying if I didn't say it was terrifying as well. Now all I had to do was find the right way to break the news to my parents.

A week or so later I went home over Easter break, and in my mind I knew it would be one of the last times I'd see my entire family for a while. I didn't choose a moment as to when to tell my parents; it more or less chose itself. It was a muggy afternoon, and I was straightening up my bedroom, my mother walked by, saw this, and laughed as she yelled out to my dad, "Vince you've got to come see this! Danny is actually cleaning up his room!" My dad showed up moments later, they made a few jokes at my expense, which were well deserved. Then as the laughter subsided, I remember a brief pause as my parents smiled at their youngest and my father said, "It's good to have you home, old boy." My mom kissed my cheek and I thought maybe this was the universe telling me that now was the perfect time to "shit or get off the pot." I tried my best to keep the mood light and was even upbeat when I told them that I was throwing caution to the wind, following my dreams, and moving to Los Angeles two weeks after graduation. Then, after an almost-knowing pause, a few obvious questions were asked by them both.

"Do you have a job?" "No, sir."

"Do you have a place to stay?" "No, ma'am."

"How much money do you have saved?" "$1,100."

"What are you going to do when you get there?" "Find a job and a place to live."

My parents weren't the overbearing types; they always encouraged me to be myself and follow my dreams. But even at this point they had to be thinking, "This is a really bad idea, even worse than the cutoff jean shorts he's wearing."

My father asked if anything in particular had happened that made me decide that this was the best course of action. I expressed to them that it was a combination of things, the biggest one being, I didn't want to wake up one day, look at my 30-year-old face in the mirror and wonder what would have happened if I ever gave LA a try. (Because at 22, 30 seems really damn old.) I knew I had to give it a shot.

I love my parents more than words, and even more for not just saying, "Son, you've got your head up your ass! You have no money, no job, nowhere to live, and no clue what the hell you're doing!" Instead, they did what good parents do. They hugged me and told me they loved me, supported my choice, and would always be there for me.

I remember that as they left my bedroom, my dad turned back and looked at me. It wasn't that "first day of high school look," it was simply honest. With a tear forming in his eye, he said, "Give 'em hell, son." He closed the door to my room and I stood in silence for a bit, then turned on the *Cinema Paradiso* soundtrack on my Panasonic Platinum boombox. I then laid on my bed and cried like a damn baby. After I'd cried it all out, I put on the song "Going the Distance" from the *Rocky* soundtrack, because I'm Italian and it's kind of what we do. At that point, I realized the hard part was over... giving them hell, that was gonna be easy!

MY FOUNDATION'S FOUNDATION

Looking back at my life, it's amazing to me that more often than not, it's been the simple moments that not only paved my path but became the directional arrows at the crossroads of my journey. At the time when they were happening, these moments might have seemed like inconsequential, matter-of-fact life blips, but they turned out to be the ones that ended up determining so much of who I've become.

For example, if I were watching my life as a movie, when one of those moments occurred, I would have thought, "Well, nothing's happening here, so I'm gonna go take a leak, refill my third bucket of unlimited popcorn, and explain my theory to the candy guy that calling Milk Duds a "dud" is doing the candy a disservice and they should be called Milk Dudes." But when I'd get back to the theater and sit down, I'd see people on the edge of their seats, laughing and crying at the same time, and the guy next to me just shaking his head and giving me his best "Bro, you freakin' missed it" face. I'm like, "What the hell is going on? What did I miss? How did this happen? So, that guy with the funky teeth and the thing with the thing was important in my life?"

Apparently, there's a reason your brain chooses to remember these times as opposed to many of the "more important ones." As I get older and continually become more aware, it's so enjoyable to piece together the puzzle of my life and finally make sense of how all of the moments fit together so perfectly. Especially those moments that initially seemed like they were just a few random, leftover pieces thrown into the box. It's important to understand and accept that each and every moment matters.

I've never lived my life saying "what if." I prefer to say "why not?" To me, "what if" is stamped with a negative label, because the majority of the time we use it to wonder "what if" a bad situation would have been better. All that does is stifle our growth and keep our mind in a place it was meant to leave behind. If you can realize and accept why certain things happen and why others don't, then you can grow from them, learn from them, and appreciate them. You can leave them behind and move on with a more positive mindset that accepts the fact that we get to where we are in life by the choices we make. We can't always control the circumstances of certain situations, but we can control how we choose to deal with those circumstances.

Who knows…if my brother decided to stay home that random autumn evening, he never would've seen Phil, I probably never would have gone to UNC, so I'd never have been in

Richard Drefuss's office, I never would have had an "in" at MTV, and therefore, maybe I would have ended up back in Wampum, PA, working at the steel mill with a black eye and a broken nose. Hey JC, thanks for taking one, or should I say drinking one, for the team.

If there was only one thing that my foundation has taught me, it's this. Work hard, be kind to others, do what's right, follow your gut, and appreciate every moment, especially the small ones. Life might not always work out the way you want it to, but it's working out the way it's supposed to. So, be aware and choose wisely. Why not?

PART 2
FAME

GO WEST, YOUNG MAN

With one portion of my life complete, I was more than ready, anxious, and excited to see what was in store for me next. I was 22 years old and so wet behind the ears my lobes had pit stains. Obviously, I was curious but also unsure what the future was holding for me. I hoped it was holding a job as well as some money, because life was about to "get real." But truthfully at that point, the only thing that mattered was, I was in L.A., baby, and I was ready to give 'em hell!

My cross-country drive came to an end with me cruising into Santa Monica on the fabled Route 66. Maybe there was some foreshadowing and irony to that, since my first acting gig would eventually land me the lead role in the NBC reboot of that storied series.

My sister helped me out with a place to stay for a minute—see if you can follow this. My sister's neighbor in Ohio supposedly had a friend who lived in Santa Monica, who had agreed to let me crash on her couch for "exactly and only one week" until I found a place of my own. She was a single woman in her late 30s whose, let's call it, quirkiness was only outmeasured by her kindness of letting a total stranger stay on her couch. With the week quickly passing by, I held true to our agreement and on day five I found myself a tiny studio apartment to call home.

Apparently, a few years after I had achieved a bit of success on MTV, the woman told her friend in Ohio, who in turn told my sister, who in turn told me, that we had "hooked up." Now, while the details of said "hooking" would probably make this story more enticing to romance novel enthusiasts and Fabio fan club members, it just wasn't true. The book would have been titled *50 Shades of No Way!* At least now maybe she can rework her story by saying something like, "Figures the guy who used to fart on my couch in his sleep would call me quirky." All I'd be able to say about that is, it holds a bit more weight than the "hooking up" story.

I was flying solo in L.A., and in my mind, my studio apartment was amazing. The building apparently hadn't been updated since the late 1960s, and if the rust-colored shag rug in my room could tell the tales of yesteryear, I'm sure they would have been saucier than Olive Garden's Fettuccine Alfredo.

The place was unfurnished so I unleashed my inner interior decorator and added a few necessities that tied everything together and really made it feel like home. First, a futon—it's not just multifaceted, it's stylish as well. It's a bed, it's a couch, no, it's a futon! (I wonder if "bouch" was ever in the discussion as a name choice). Next, a hot plate. Stoves can be cumbersome, but a hot plate does the same job in a tenth of the space, leaving so much more room for activities. Finally, a bright yellow, dual-cassette-deck Sony boombox. R.I.P. Panasonic Platinum, but this was L.A. and I needed to look the part as well.

In my mind, this place might as well have been The Four Seasons, and I felt like I was livin' large in L.A. (Sorry, but I had to use "livin' large" as an homage to overused 90s phrases gone too soon.) Unfortunately, thanks to the down payment on the studio and the futon purchase, my $1,100 was fading faster than Snoop Dogg on a Friday night.

Thus, the job hunt was on. I was open to anything I could find that would pay the bills and put food on my TV tray. Don't worry I didn't buy the TV tray. I found that little treasure left in the closet. It was good as new once I scrubbed the stains off of it. First things first, I reached out to the MTV peeps in New York to see if they were going to be shooting anything in L.A. I let them know that I was ready to work, but to no avail. Honestly, I think they probably got tired of me calling after a while.

Luckily a few blocks away from my place was a bar/grill I'd frequent called Mom's Saloon. It was a hole-in-the-wall kind of place that was pretty popular with the UCLA students because the burgers were cheap and the pitchers were cheaper. I became friendly with the manager after having hung out there a few times, so I hit him up for a bartending gig. I guess he liked me enough that morning or was still drunk from the night prior, so he hired me.

With the job box checked, I was clinging to my mantra, "It's all about the tips," because this place would get packed on the weekends. When I inquired about what shift I'd be working, he replied "Shift? Shit dude, it's almost a two-year wait to bartend here. You're working the door." This was a blow to my bartending ego, but more than likely it was karma with a sly smirk and a kick to my stones after all of the free shots and beers I gave away in Chapel Hill.

But I stayed positive. It was still a job, and maybe I could put my Downtown Julie Brown bodyguard techniques to work at the door. The gig was basically this: I only got paid $3.75 an hour, but the hook was, for every fake ID I found I'd get $20 cash at the end of the night. So as time went on and rent needed to be paid, I started taking legitimate IDs from of-age college kids just so I could make a few extra bucks. Each time I chose to do it, I'd make sure it was either a guy who was smaller than me or a girl who was with a group of friends who wanted to party. Then, I'd put my remedial acting skills to the test and I'd attempt to make it sound like I was doing them a favor.

"Look I'm going to let you in the bar, but I'm gonna need to keep the ID because its legitimacy is questionable. If it is real, just come back tomorrow at noon and pick it up." I always thought by saying "legitimacy is questionable," it made my legitimacy seem less questionable. College kids surprisingly didn't care; they just wanted to get inside and start drinking. Especially the girls. "Krissy, he's letting you in, just come back and get it tomorrow. Plus, Becky's got Fireball shots waiting." Honestly, I did feel bad because they were basically my age, but I needed the money. I mean, what good is having a hot plate if you can't afford the mac n' cheese to cook on it?

A week or so later, I headed into the bar to have lunch and my manager approached me. I saw the look on his face. He knew, and I knew he knew. He told me that kids kept coming in to pick up real IDs that I'd confiscated, and then he asked how much money I had on me. I'd just come from the ATM where I'd taken out my money for the week, $40. Isn't it amazing when you're young, how long you can stretch money out for?

Anyway, I told him I had $42. He said, "Give me $40 and keep the other two." I did as I was told and then watched him put the $40 into his own wallet. He proceeded to walk behind the bar, filled a pitcher of beer, brought it back, and sat it on the table right in front of me and said, "If I catch you doing it again, you're fired." As he walked off, all that I thought was, "Sweet, a free pitcher of beer and I still have a job. This is a good day!" I've always been a positive, glass-half-full kind of guy, but when a pitcher is totally full, my positivity is off the charts.

When I got home a bit later, I collapsed on my futon, ate the remains of some stale Goldfish crackers, and checked my answering machine. The red light was blinking, one message. "Hi, this message is for Dan. My name is Ted Demme and I'm the producer of *Yo! MTV Raps* . . . " That's all I heard, because in my rush to sit up and listen (because as men we think we hear better when we sit up) I started choking on a freakin' Goldfish. I think part of it is still lodged deep inside my nasal cavity. (That would definitely explain why, even to this day, I still taste a hint of synthetic cheddar every time I sneeze.) Ted said he was coming to L.A. to shoot an episode of *Yo!* and they needed a P.A. (production assistant) for the shoot. I obviously returned the call and happily accepted the job. A two-day shoot, $75/day, yep, that definitely bought a helluva lot of mac n' cheese and fresh Goldfish.

Not only was I happy to be working, I was a huge fan of *Yo! MTV Raps*. Recognizing the potential opportunity, I busted my ass to make everything as perfect as I possibly could for that shoot. Thankfully, I think Ted appreciated it because after that, I became *Yo's* go-to P.A. when they shot in L.A. We had shoots all over the city—the L.A. River, Ice Cube's house, Ice T's house, and all the other ice houses. Thankfully no Ice Castles, or else I would have had to make sure not to forget about the roses...(that one was for the white kids from the early 80s). The shoot at Ice T's house was the first time I ever saw a money counter, massive stacks of cash, guns, and weed all on a desk at the same time. Actually, it was the only time I ever saw that, but what a glorious time it was. God bless MTV in the 90s.

FROM FULL TIME TO PRIME TIME

Times were good, but I kept envisioning them getting better. I was still working the door at Mom's Saloon, but with these occasional MTV gigs picking up, I was not only thrilled but I could feel the roots of my life in L.A. starting to firmly plant themselves. My mindset was simply to work as hard as possible, be as positive as possible, and the rest would take care of itself. The wetness behind my ears was now closer to morning dew at this point.

The hard work I put in at *Yo!* definitely paid off and because of it, I started working for other New York–based MTV shows that would occasionally shoot in L.A. That spring, another moment occurred that helped to push me further along on my journey. MTV decided to open up offices on the West Coast. The initial office was tiny, less than 10 people, but they were going to need full-time office P.A.s and I was fortunate enough to land one of those two spots.

It was actually a wonderful time in my life. I had a full-time job working for MTV, I was making a steady $300 a week, and I was rockin' the sickest used Toyota Corolla FX hatchback in Hollywood—a sweet five-speed, because apparently four speeds just wasn't enough, that had more miles on it than Hugh Hefner at the Playboy Mansion grotto. Its character was firmly enhanced by the sun-faded and chipped red paint, which I would always describe as "having an iridescent flare." Its tires were almost too thin to put on a ten-speed Schwinn, and any time I'd drive over 40 mph it would rattle worse than a Yahtzee dice cup. Obviously, the rattling had to be fixed. I was no mechanic, but I knew what to do. I installed a used Kraco stereo under the dash and turned it up to 11 every time I drove. Now the rattling just seemed like a cool subwoofer bonus feature. Problem solved.

Having an office in Los Angeles meant that MTV would start producing original content on the West Coast, and I was fortunate to be a part of that as well. Some of the show's I worked on were classics like *Headbanger's Ball*, *Totally Pauly*, *The Big Picture*, and *Rockline* with the one and only O.G. VJ, Martha Quinn. Anyone who grew up watching MTV needs to know Martha is one of the nicest people you could ever meet. Yes, she's crazy talented, but more so than that, she was kind to everyone, from the biggest bosses to the lowliest of P.As, i.e., me. In a bizarre sort of MTV universe irony, we've also been neighbors in Malibu for the last 20 years, and if you're curious, yes, she still looks like she's 25 . . . and I still get her coffee for her.

VITAL
IDOL

There were a few rather defining moments throughout my days as a P.A. at MTV, and this one definitely left a rock n' roll imprint on my brain. It was March 1, 1991, and Oliver Stone's much anticipated and controversial biopic, *The Doors*, was about to hit the big screen. That night we were shooting the premiere party for the film from the world-famous Whisky a Go-Go on the fabled Sunset Strip. MTV was airing the much-publicized event as a live special.

Performing for the show was none other than rock n' roll rebel Billy Idol. I was, as I said at the time, "jacked up beyond belief" to be working the show. I mean, to be inside the historic Whisky, which just oozed rock n' roll folklore, and to see Billy Idol perform was a pretty decent night's work.

My job description for the evening was as follows: Take $200 petty cash, go a block away to the liquor store, and buy enough adult beverages to make Billy Idol, Billy "Fucking" Idol. Then prep his dressing room with all of the goodies. Didn't seem so hard, but it turned out to be a bit more difficult than I anticipated. I mean, what do rock stars really drink? I was 22 and on a tight budget. I had no clue what to get. At the time I was drinking 40s of Schlitz with the occasional shot of Jåeger when I felt like splurging. Billy was British and just didn't really strike me as a malt liquor kind of guy. So I bought what I thought a millionaire rock star would drink: two cases of Heineken and as much champagne as the petty cash would allow.

When I went to pay, the guy working behind the counter asked me what the occasion was, so I told him the truth. "I'm buying drinks for Billy Idol." He side-eyed me for a second, then said, "Well, if I were you, I'd trade out a lot of that champagne for vodka." He spoke with such conviction that even through his thick accent, he sounded like he knew what he was talking about. So, I agreed and made the vodka swap, plus I threw in a couple bags of potato chips, some M&M's (because supposedly rock stars like them in their dressing rooms), and a can of mixed nuts, just in case he was feeling posh.

When I got back to the Whisky, I hurried upstairs and did my best to get Billy's dressing room rock-star ready. Oddly enough, I remember being really proud of myself for including the mixed nuts—why wouldn't I be? I mean, nothing says "crazy and classy" all at once quite like mixed nuts. Once his room was good to go, I received my marching orders from downstairs via my walkie talkie. "Just wait for Billy. When he gets here, do whatever he needs you to do and get him anything he asks for."

So, I followed my orders and literally sat on a folding chair to the left of the dressing room door, anxiously waiting for Billy Idol to arrive. Trust me, if social media would have existed at the time, my Insta feed would have been blowing up with obnoxious pre-Idol-waiting selfies. But it didn't, so it was just me sitting there alone, sweating my ass off in this tiny little hallway with the smell of cigarettes and booze oozing from the pores of the wooden floors.

I could hear the buzz from the excited crowd downstairs as they filed in and began to party. At least that's what it sounded like from my rather solitary vantage point. Truthfully, I couldn't even feel my legs, thanks to the shitty old folding chair cutting off the blood circulation from my ass to my feet. So I very easily could have been hallucinating.

After what seemed like an eternity, I got the call on my walkie, "They're here, Billy's heading up!" Holy shit! I was nervous as hell! How do I make the intro and let him know what I'm doing here? More importantly, how do I regain feeling in my legs? I heard the backdoor downstairs swing open, and the sounds and energy to follow were only similar to what I experienced when I ran with the bulls in Pamplona, Spain.

What seemed to be like a hundred boot-covered feet started hustling up the creaking wooden steps, people were cheering, girls giggling, guys somehow laughing and yelling profanities simultaneously. Was there a ventriloquist with him, how do they do that? As they got closer to me, I did my best to stand up so I could introduce myself. I still couldn't see anyone, but it felt like their pace was rapidly picking up. The tingling in my legs from the blood returning to them was almost painful. I was trying to shake them out before everyone reached me, because God forbid they got there as I was doing it and the first impression Billy Idol had of me was me doing the fucking Hokey Pokey outside of his dressing room door.

Then the flood gates finally opened. As they reached the top of the steps, the entourage began pouring in. The first one I saw was a behemoth of a tattooed man, followed by a pack of skinny rocker-type guys with cigarettes dangling from their lips, and mixed throughout—almost as if for an 80s rock video—was a plethora of scantily clad girls that very easily could have been the mainstage all-stars at the Body Shop. Surrounded by a separate individual harem of girls and followed by a tiny Hollywood-looking agent type in a suit was Billy Idol. The crew was then bookended with another fucking huge tattooed guy. (Sorry, I just felt it wasn't really appropriate to use *behemoth* twice, since the last time was the first time I've ever used it.)

In the midst of this Flesh for Fantasy stampede, I tried to get out the words, "Hi, I'm Dan with MTV. Let me know if you need anything." The truth of the matter being, I think all I got out was, "Oh sorry, my bad. Let me get out of the way." Once everyone was inside, the door to the dressing room slammed behind them with an echo acting as a do-not-disturb exclamation point. Just like that, I was alone again in the tiny hallway, only now not only did I hear music and the crowd partying downstairs, but I could also hear the good time of Billy and The Idolettes muffled right behind the door next to me. It was almost like I was on some sort of game show and I had to figure out what was going on behind Door Number One.

As showtime rapidly approached, I received numerous calls on my walkie from the important people in charge downstairs inquiring how everything was going. Trying to keep it together, I'd reply with lame quips like, "We're all cool up here," with the hopes that my coworkers on the other end of the walkie would believe I was somehow letting my freak flag fly with Billy and his posse.

Then I heard something from inside the dressing room. I wasn't sure at first, but it sounded like someone with a British accent was screaming, "MTV!" Then it happened again, over and over, "MTV! MTV!" I wasn't sure what to do. Were they calling me, or was this some kind of preshow drinking game that rock stars do? For example, if he were performing in London, would they be screaming "BBC! BBC!"?

Next thing I knew, the door to the dressing room flew open and scared the shit out of me so badly that it almost scared the shit out of me! I immediately jumped up, and just as quickly my legs started to tingle again. I think all of the blood rushing to them was leaving my head, because it was accompanied by that combination of muffled hearing and high-pitched ringing you get right before you pass out.

One of the giant guys was standing there looking down on me like I was a Keebler elf. He barked, "MTV, we've been calling you!" I'm pretty sure my response was something close to a *Beavis and Butthead*-esque "uhhhh 'kay." He lifted his giant hands, put them to my chest, each one was holding a bottle of the bubbly, and bellowed, "Billy doesn't drink champagne."

The door slammed behind him before I could reply with another rousing rendition of "uhhh 'kay." As I sat back down I remember thinking how cool it all was. I mean, sure I wasn't partying with Billy Idol, but was this a potential ice breaker? In my mind, I was on the threshold of potentially getting called in for a drink at any second. Believe me when I say, for a kid who was shining shoes in Pittsburgh a few years earlier, this was like winning the lottery. Yep, I was just putting that positivity out into the Universe. Glass half full and champagne bottle totally full.

Lost in the thoughts of all of my unrealistic expectations, I got another call on my walkie, "We go live in two minutes. Let Billy know." "Copy that." I took a deep breath, got up from my chair, straightened my MTV t-shirt, briefly hesitated, then knocked on Billy's dressing room door. Looking back, it was probably more of a light tap than a knock. There was no response from inside. All I heard was that laughter and profanity mixture, girls squealing, and a lot of "Oh my God's."

A shouting voice on the other end of the walkie "Ninety seconds, how's he doing?" I shouted back, "He's ready to rock!" Not sure why I said that, but it sounded kind of appropriate under the circumstances. Then right before I knocked again, I heard the band on stage downstairs starting to play the opening organ lick of The Doors, "Touch Me." The drunken crowd began losing their minds in anticipation of Billy taking the stage any second. So my knock this time was a bit more assertive, followed by a quasi-authoritative "Live in 90 seconds." As those words were leaving my lips my walkie simultaneously screamed "One minute, one minute and we are live!" To which I raised my voice outside the door saying "One minute!" Unfortunately, when it came out it sounded more like a prepubescent teen doing a poor *Saved by the Bell* Screech imitation.

The organ "Touch Me" lick was playing over and over, seemingly getting louder with every loop. Over the walkie, "Where the hell is Billy? Is everything okay?" to which I responded, "On his way!" I finally girded my loins, knocked like a man, and said, "This is MTV! We go live in less than a minute!"

The response I got was not shocking because there was none. It was at this moment I did what anyone in my situation would do, I decided to check the sweat stains under my arms. As I raised my arm to check the stains, my hand hit my walkie knocking it off of my belt, sending it crashing to the floor.

The music and crowd noise from downstairs both kept increasing in volume. I felt like I was in the middle of a Paul Thomas Anderson movie. By the time I clipped my walkie back on my belt and picked up my earpiece, all I heard was what sounded like a hundred people screaming, "WE ARE LIVE, WE ARE LIVE! WHERE'S BILLY?" Off of those words, with one fluid motion, I opened the dressing room door, being sure to keep my eyes to the floor and yelled, "WE ARE LIVE!" Then I quickly closed the door and listened closely, kind of like when someone who cracks a safe combination does.

Seconds later, the dressing room door flew open and out ran the rocker-type dudes and the girls, followed by one of the giant guys. It was madness. I proudly yelled into my walkie, "Billy's on his way to stage!" The only problem was, the door slammed closed behind the big guy, and no Billy. The band kept getting louder downstairs. At this point, apparently, my walkie had been rendered useless, because someone screamed from the bottom of the steps, "Dan! We've been live, where the fuck is Billy?!" In my mind, I responded, "I know! Now shut the fuck up, you tool!" But the rock n' roll gods were smiling down on me and I didn't need to respond. Because at that moment the dressing room door swung open and out rolled the other huge guy followed by Billy. As he walked by, in badass rock-star fashion, he backhanded me to the chest, gave me his patented sneer, and said "MTV!" Hopefully my swoon wasn't audible, but it was official, me and Billy were buds.

Then he hustled down the steps to the stage, not because he knew we'd been live—I think he enjoyed that part—but because he was just amped and ready to go. Billy reached the stage, the crowd went apeshit, and he seemlessly picked up his cue from the band and sang, "Come on, come on, come on, come on and FUCK me baby!" Amazing how changing one word in a song on live television sends a network into mayhem.

I knew my job was more or less done until the end of the show, so I took one of the bottles of champagne from under my chair, went halfway down the stairs, sat down, popped the cork, and watched Billy Idol crush it.

As the show was coming to an end, I went back up to my position by the dressing room. With the band still playing and the crowd going crazy, Billy ran up the steps with one of the girls in tow and as they ran past me, like a true rock star, he snagged the champagne bottle from my hand, kicked the back door open, and they left.

Over my walkie I heard someone yelling, "Does anyone have eyes on Billy?" I ran to the back door of the Whisky and opened it just in time to see Billy pulling away on his Harley. His girl was on the back—she was holding him tight with one hand and slamming champagne with the other.

Then in one of the coolest rock-star moments of my life, I stood alone at the backdoor and proceeded to watch him peel tire out of the parking lot and turn left down Sunset Boulevard. As he drove out of sight, I could still hear the muffler in the distance and I remember thinking, I guess I did my job, because the guy who's rolling down Sunset Boulevard right now is, without a doubt, Billy "Fucking" Idol.

NOT QUITE AN OVERNIGHT SENSATION

It was September 1991 and I was in the midst of living my MTV production assistant dreams. With my $300 per week paycheck, unlimited access to MTV swag, and a basement apartment in Manhattan Beach, I was living the life. That was, until the day the hammer dropped—or should I say, began to drop.

I was told that word had come down from MTV headquarters in New York that, due to certain corporate words my brain has chosen to forget, the MTV L.A. office would be experiencing "cutbacks." Which loosely translated to, "Hey, Dan, since you're basically the new guy and expendable, as of the first of the year you're being let go." I don't remember being too distraught, as I had heard rumblings of this potentially happening. Also, January seemed light years away from September. Again, there's something to be said for the naiveté of a 23-year-old with a few, very few, dollars in his pocket.

The rest of September and into October was business as usual for me. I hadn't even looked for a job, but in fact I tried to be proactive and come up with a way to not only keep mine but improve upon it. I guess the bold choice to start using a hair dryer on my West Coast mullet was actually drying out the wet area behind my ears, because I decided to hand in a treatment for a show idea I'd had for a while. I wanted to create a show that would not only cover mainstream sports but all the crazy extreme sports I was introduced to when I moved to the West Coast. I not only wanted to produce it but host it as well. It was called *MTV: Sport This!* It was greeted with great promise by the head of the L.A. office, Paul Cockerill, who in turn forwarded the idea to the big dogs in New York, where it was said to have "heat" around it for a while. Apparently, that "heat" turned out more of a low-grade fever, because after the first week it was radio silence regarding the idea.

Jump to mid-November when one of the network's West Coast talent executives approached me with a rather poignant question, "Hey Dan, you're really into sports, who do you think would be good to host this new sports show we're doing?" When I inquired more about her question, she proceeded to tell me that it was a new show based around extreme sports called *MTV Sports* and the search for the host was on the fast track. I was adamant that not only was that my idea but I should at the very least be given an opportunity to audition for it. She dismissed my claim by saying it would be relatively impossible for me to prove the idea was mine since there were a number of similar ideas floating around the New York office.

Truth was, at that time I didn't care whose idea it was; I just wanted a shot at hosting it. So I pleaded again for a chance to at least audition for the gig. What she said after that was something many would consider a harsh life lesson, but it turned out to be a moment from which I learned so much and for which I will forever be thankful. She looked at me very matter of factly and said, "They'll never let you host. You're too ethnic to be on television."

Now where I grew up, it was a badge of honor to be "ethnic." If you don't believe me, I've got quite a few Pisans from the 'Burgh who will back me up on that one.

So I asked her to clarify what she meant, and she again very bluntly replied, "No one wants to watch a white guy trying to be a black guy ... and that's what you are." Then she walked away, leaving me standing there a bit taken aback. I mean, I heard what she said, but it made no sense to me. I had never tried to be anyone or anything that I wasn't, I'd always been proud just being me. When I got home later that evening, I remember thinking how I couldn't let such a flaccid excuse deter me from a potentially amazing opportunity. I was just unsure how to go about getting it. The following is how the chance at getting that opportunity unfolded.

Monday

I believe it was a week or so later, and the day had arrived. The auditions for the *MTV Sports* hosting finalists was taking place at a local studio where we used to shoot several shows. Over the preceding days, I had repeatedly asked Paul, the head of our West Coast office, for a shot at the gig, to which he would always reply, "We'll see, Dan." The list of 10 to 15 finalists was made up of professional surfers and volleyball players—basically, cool beach dudes with name cache. I was neither a cool beach dude nor the proud owner of any type of cache or even cash for that matter.

In the midst of diligently attending to my P.A. duties in the control room, I heard someone mention that one of the finalists was running late. With this, Paul yelled in my direction, "Hey Dan, I don't want to wait, so if you think you can do this, run out to stage and go for it." I wasn't sure if he was serious, but I did know that Paul was a fair guy, so I hustled my "ethnic" ass out onto the stage.

When I entered, I was greeted by cheers from the three cameramen whom I knew. The response from the talent executive was basically the polar opposite. She was less than pleased to see the "P.A. from down the hall" standing in front of her on stage. During the audition process, the candidates would take their mark on camera, she'd ask them questions, and their responses would be filmed. When I stepped onto my mark, she refused to ask me anything, because in her eyes I wasn't worthy of the audition.

Therefore, I was left with no other choice than to do what I did best, so I started talking and didn't stop. The fact is, her not asking me questions put me in charge of the audition, because now I could say whatever I felt like saying, and I did just that, as I spoke directly into the lens of each camera. But I wasn't talking to the camera, I was talking to the people operating them, thus giving the viewer a name and a purpose and in doing so, making them become part of the process with me. People have asked me if this was something that I'd planned out prior or if it was intentional. I wish, but the answer is no. That was just what I was told by executives who had watched the tape later. I was nervous and had no time to think, so I was just letting it fly and trying to be me. Plus, I wasn't even sure if they were recording me, so in the heat of the moment I did a little improv about going mud wrestling with the camera crew.

Then after a minute or two, I heard over the stage intercom, "Dan, the guy's here. Get off the stage." I exited to a smattering of applause mixed with laughs from the crew and went back to my P.A. duties. At the end of that day, I went home with tons of mixed emotions. I was excited for the opportunity but was unsure if I was even filmed, and if so, did they even add it to the reel? Ironically, the person in charge of overnighting all of the footage to New York was me.

Tuesday

The next afternoon, I was sitting in my office and I got a call from New York. *MTV Sports* über executive producer Patrick Byrnes was on the other end of the line. Apparently, my audition was tacked on to the end of the reel sent to the MTV brass in NYC. As Patrick proceeded to tell me how much he liked my audition, I clapped back with some sort of lame, unfunny retort like "Yeah, okay," because truthfully I didn't believe it was Patrick, I thought it was my friend Ed Capuano pranking me.

Patrick reassured me that he was definitely the one on the other end of the line. Then he proceeded to explain that he felt what really separated me from everyone else who auditioned was my energy and that I was just being myself. He continued, saying they were planning on shooting the pilot episode that upcoming Saturday at the New River Gorge in West Virginia. Then he very calmly finished the conversation by saying, "What do you say? Do you want to be the host of *MTV Sports*?"

Truthfully, I don't remember what my response was, but obviously there was a "yes" mixed somewhere in the midst of all of my blabbering. One thing I do remember and always will, is that he said I got the job because I was different and that he felt I was just being myself. Not a guy who was "too ethnic" or "a white guy trying to be a black guy" or a plaid guy trying to be pin-striped one. I was just Dan. Since that day, something I've always try to remind myself no matter what the situation: Words can only *describe* who you are, your actions **define** who you are—and because of those actions, I was the host of *MTV Sports*!

Wednesday

I received my hosting contract via fax machine (remember those?). New York needed a quick response, so my goal was to try and find someone, anyone, with any type of legal knowledge to look it over for me. But to no avail. So, I did the next best thing, I passed it around the office to see what my coworkers thought. The most common responses I got were "cool" and "sweet." Now, I'd never taken the bar exam but I was pretty sure those were not common legal terms. Because of this I decided what I needed to do was go over it again myself, then sleep on it and pray that years of watching *People's Court* would somehow enlighten me with the necessary legal knowledge the following morning.

Thursday

When I got to work that morning, I had a voice message from someone in MTV's business affairs department informing me that if the contract wasn't signed and faxed back to New York by noon PST, that they were moving on with a different host. So obviously, I asked myself, "What would Wopner do?" then I immediately signed it and sent the contract back to New York.

The one thing that people who aren't in the entertainment industry always assume is that if you're on a TV show, you're not only making bank, you're making BIG bank. By placing my signature on that faded faxed contract that day, I went from making $300 per week as a production assistant to making $400 per episode as host of *MTV Sports*...and no, that was not a typo. I would occasionally tell people my bank was big, but what I didn't tell them was, it was a piggy bank. More on that later.

After signing the contract, I left work early to buy a few necessities for my trip to West Virginia the following day. Since I had to supply my own wardrobe, I knew there were two things I definitely had to have. Cut to, Manhattan Beach Mall parking lot and my Toyota Corolla hatchback coming to a rattling halt, topped off with a tiny tire screech.

My first purchase was a no-brainer, a new earring. There was no way I was going to wear my fake diamond stud on MTV. Plus, just imagine if the "gold plating" turned my ear lobe green again while we were shooting. Not a good look for day one on the job. The problem at that moment was, I felt more than a little out of place in the ladies' costume jewelry department at Macy's. I had the look of a sixteen-year-old trying to buy condoms at Costco, but then something amazing happened. They say lightning only strikes the same place once, but I think it's twice. Because what stopped me dead in my tracks were two "gold" hooped earrings with a lightning bolt dangling from each one. To me, they screamed equal parts sophistication and rock n' roll, but what they really screamed was, "These are potentially the lamest earrings of all time!"

With the earring box checked, I swiftly moved on for my next purchase, a three-pack of new bandannas. Nothing shined a light on the sweet marriage of 90s grunge and gangsta like wearing a bandanna. Over the years, it actually became known as my signature MTV look. While many people believed it was a conscious choice of mine in helping to create my brand, that wasn't entirely true. The main reason I started wearing them was mostly to look cool, but running a close second was out of vanity. I used to think that the lines on my forehead were not only unsymmetrical, but that they looked worse than Jimmy Superfly Snuka's forehead after a cage match with Rowdy Roddy Piper. Hence, the perfect solution, a bandanna aka the Dandanna to cover the irregularity and put all of my forehead insecurities to rest. Armed with lightning bolts, bandannas, and all the boxes checked, I was ready to bring my "A" game to the MTV masses.

Friday

After three coach-class connections and approximately 20 bags of airplane peanuts, I arrived in Fayetteville, West Virginia, in the early evening. I immediately headed for the town of Victor, home of the New River Gorge Bridge. You feel like you're away from everything when you're there, because you *really* are. But it's some of the most beautiful countryside in the land. I think we stayed at a Quality Inn and, thanks to lessons learned in the past, I did not check in between the mattresses.

There I met up with the crew, made up of a few people I knew from the New York office, as well as executive producer, Patrick Byrnes. We had a few beers and brief production meeting in anticipation of the pilot shoot the following morning.

Saturday

October 19, 1991. A beautiful, crisp autumn morning, the crew, my lightning bolt earring, and bandanna-covered forehead all arrived ready to create something special. You're probably wondering, why West Virginia, why the New River Gorge Bridge? I mean admittedly, they don't really scream "MTV," but that day they did. We were there to cover Bridge Day, an annual event where BASE jumpers, bungee jumpers, and repellers gather from around the globe to jump their crazy asses off of a perfectly good bridge 876 feet above the ground. After witnessing this event in person, trust me, there could not have been a better or more "extreme" event to cover for the pilot episode of the most extreme sports show ever made.

During the course of shooting tons of footage and interacting with the jumpers and thousands of fans in attendance, I remember Patrick asking me if I'd want to try BASE jumping off of the bridge for the show. I said "Sure," because I didn't have the intestinal fortitude to say, "Um, hell no!" and also because I didn't want to be fired two hours into the job. We, in turn, met with our BASE jumping expert who needed to ask me a few questions prior to jumping. "Dan, have you ever BASE jumped before?" "No." "Have you ever been skydiving before?" "No." "Have you ever bungee jumped before?" "No."

His response was something along the lines of, "Yeah, I don't think it would be a real good idea for Dan to jump today." On the inside I was cheering like a kid at Christmas. On the outside, I masked my excitement with an "Aww man, that sucks." Crisis averted, manhood still intact as my balls slowly dropped back down into their natural position.

The rest of the shoot could not have gone better because it didn't feel like we were working or even filming a television show. It just felt like we were a small group of friends who were doing some crazy stuff and just decided to film it for ourselves to laugh at later.

Looking back at the show, it was that attitude we all had that helped to create the irreverence of the series. We were never too concerned whether viewers would think what we were doing was cool. It was always based on whether *we* thought it was cool. I've always felt that this honest passion repeatedly came across in the finished product of every episode, and that was what made the show cool.

Sunday

For some reason, the three-layover return flight and pounds of airplane peanuts seemed more like first class this time. That evening, I returned to my basement apartment in Manhattan Beach and it almost seemed like the shoot was a dream. No one traveled back with me because the show was produced out of New York, so the crew all returned home to the Big Apple.

I recall sitting on my futon, popping open an MGD and thinking about where my life was just one week earlier. I realized how blessed I was to have been placed in situations where opportunities presented themselves and thankful for being raised with the awareness to recognize when those opportunities arose. I truly believed at that moment that *MTV Sports* not only had a chance to be special, but that it would provide a platform for me to attempt to do so as well.

BO KNOWS, BUT BO DOESN'T KNOW DAN

On the heels of living and breathing BASE jumping insanity at Bridge Day, we then had to finish up the pilot of *MTV Sports* by filming some wrap-around segments. They were basically going to be threaded throughout the show to tie all the other bits and pieces together. The initial concept for the series was to do the wrap-arounds with an athlete or celebrity in a more controlled interview environment, so basically a more traditional sit-down interview in a studio with them.

Luckily, the very first guest we got was probably the greatest athlete on the planet at the time of our shoot, Bo Jackson. I could not have been more excited, especially since Bo was at the peak of his career, playing both professional football and baseball, but thanks to Nike's "Bo Knows" campaign, he was at the height of the American pop culture ladder as well.

Bo actually wasn't even slated to be our first guest, but thanks to some brilliant casting maneuvering by Patrick Byrnes, we were able to get him for thirty minutes after he was done filming a video countdown show on another stage. Our set was simple. We had a couch and, well, it was just the couch. A couch randomly perched alone in the middle of a huge stage like Gilligan's Island, just patiently waiting for Bo and I to sit down and talk. We were also shooting the segment on 16 mm black and white film, which to me felt extremely professional, or as my friends in Pittsburgh would say, "artsie fartsie." I wouldn't say I was nervous, but Bo was notorious for being a very serious man of very few words. The intimacy of our set aided in making my task of getting him to open up and show the lighter side of himself a rather difficult one.

Bo was running late from the other shoot, so I tried to keep myself loose and the crew entertained with some juvenile humor guaranteed to get laughs, even if the laughs were just my own. At one point I remember calling out "Bo knows? Really? Okay, I'll tell you what Bo don't know, Bo don't know Dan!" Crickets. Not as much as a snicker or even a smirk, but rather blank stares all around. Feeling a presence behind me, I turned toward the back entrance of the stage and there stood Bo Jackson, backlit by the sunlight coming in through the open door behind him.

For a long beat, everyone just looked at him, and then, like something out of a horror film, the creaking door slowly closed behind him. Patrick and others hustled over to him. I made my way over to Bo as well after I took my foot out of my mouth, which wasn't so easy considering how far I had my head up my ass.

As I approached him I remember thinking how solid he looked. Now, "solid" might seem like a silly adjective to use to describe the man, but it was true, he was like a 6'1", 230-pound block of solid granite...with the inability to smile...at me. I introduced myself and proceeded to shake his hand. I was always taught that when you shake a man's hand, you look him in the eye and make it a firm shake, so I proudly went with that approach. Bo, in turn, squeezed my hand so hard that I may or may not have farted. Hence, the reason I offered to quickly get him out of that general vicinity because I wanted to "show him the set."

We had less than five minutes of small talk, or in Bo's case small listen, before we started to shoot, and not one smile even came close to emanating from his face. Next thing I knew, Patrick called "action," the cameras began to roll, and I had no other choice but to wing it and hope for the best. "How's it going, handsome?" Apparently by "wing it" I had meant "kiss up." Bo gave me a brief quizzical stare, and at that moment I knew he was going to walk off the set. He then leaned forward and, following a surprisingly friendly smile and laugh, he said, "I'm good, man." Boom, just like that we were off and running (Figure 13.1). The relaxed back and forth between the two of us worked perfectly. Not only was this a pretty damn cool shoot, it was one of my favorites from the series. Who knew Bo was such a personable guy? Bo "freakin'" Jackson knew, that's who.

A few minutes after we wrapped, Bo approached me and said, "That was a lot of fun. Thanks for making it easy." Still to this day, that's one of the greatest compliments I'd ever been given, because one, it came from Bo Jackson, and two, I learned so much from it. That interview acted as my blueprint for every other celebrity interview I would do after that. Never ask them about things like controversy, legal issues, or contract disputes, only positivity from beginning to end. There were plenty of talented reporters around to ask those types of questions, and truthfully, I didn't care about the answers to them. I just attempted to treat every celebrity like they were someone I knew my entire life, and as cliché as it sounds, like I would want to be treated.

FIGURE 13.1 Bo's shades were $200, mine were $9 Venice Beach specials.

Prior to shooting, I always made it a point to tell anyone and everyone who was ever on camera with me to relax because at worst, this was going to be fun and easy. Plus, if anyone was going to be made fun of, it would be me. I was a big boy—not only could I take it, I encouraged it, and that became an extremely successful formula for me. Because as I've told many people over the years regarding how I work, I talk to the biggest stars on the planet the same way I talk to someone off the street. I'm not an expert on any one thing, but I know enough about everything to have a conversation with anyone about anything.

Just as in life, if people sense that you're being real with them on camera, they will reciprocate. It was me just being me, an average guy who wanted people to share in the joy and fun that I got from doing my job. Maybe in doing so, these celebrities got to show the viewers a side of themselves that had never been seen before.

ROCK N' JOCK N' TALKIN'

A few weeks after filming with Bo, we were set to shoot episode two of *MTV Sports*, but this one had a bit of a twist. We were filming my wrap-arounds from the *3rd Annual Rock n' Jock Softball Challenge*, a pro/celebrity softball game that had more stars than Michael Spinks's eyes after Iron Mike Tyson dropped him.

My man Patrick Byrnes was executive producing the *Rock n' Jock* special and was stressed out having to deal with the logistics of the shoot and egos of the celebs, so he decided to take a leap of faith. He said he wouldn't be able to simultaneously produce my wrap-arounds as well as the game, so he gave me a sheet of paper with specific talking points he wanted me to mention while I was filming. Then he sent me off by myself with the camera crew. As Patrick headed off to deal with more *Rock n' Jock* drama, he yelled back to me, "Dano, don't let me down." Hearing him say that was the equivalent of a coach's pregame pep talk. Knowing that he had that type of faith in me after shooting just one episode inspired me to *not* let him down. Once Patrick had gone, I remember there was some nervous laughter between myself and the camera crew when we realized we were on our own to shoot the wrap-arounds however we wanted to. It was similar to when your parents leave you and your brother home alone and tell you to "behave."

Before we started shooting I remembered there was one thing I had to do, per some MTV execs in New York. They had seen some of the rough footage we shot at Bridge Day and came to the conclusion that I needed to wear makeup when I was on camera. I probably needed it off camera as well, but they knew I'd potentially scoff at that idea.

Now, wearing makeup is a common occurrence on every television and movie set, but those sets also have money to pay makeup artists to apply said makeup. We did not. I mean, I wasn't even supplied wardrobe for my show, so why would they pay for a makeup artist? Not to worry, as I had the solution. Prior to the shoot, I stopped by CVS and picked up what I thought would be the appropriate makeup needed for the day. Plus, I bought some bubblegum and condoms just so they didn't think I was some guy alone, only buying makeup. I had to keep my manhood intact with the CVS checkers.

Anyway, I told my cameraman I had to quickly do something before we could start shooting. There were no bathrooms in sight, so I popped into one of the Port-a-Johns that were there for the Rock n' Jock game, pulled out my Almay Tawny Beige foundation and commenced to getting my face "camera ready."

Having never applied makeup before, I wasn't sure if there was a proper way to do it, so I went with what I felt was the best method. I poured an ample amount into my hands, vigorously rubbed them together and applied it all over my face as if it was sunscreen. The Port-a John I was in wasn't one of those hoity-toity ones with a plastic mirror, so I had to estimate how evenly I was applying all of the tawny beige beauty to my face.

Once I was finished and ready for my close up, I headed back out to my camera crew, and I remember the two of them just staring at me for a long beat. My cameraman broke the silence by saying in a hushed tone, "Dude, what the hell is on your face?" to which I rather nonchalantly responded, "What do you mean?" He followed it with another vote of confidence by saying, "Your call, but if I were you, I'd go and take that shit off. You look like you were playing in a mud puddle."

Thankfully, there was a water fountain nearby so I could attempt to remove all of the mud puddle tawny goodness. I used one hand to hold the handle down and the other to splash water on my face like people do in the movies when they've been stuck in the desert for three weeks. Unfortunately, they didn't supply towels at the water fountain, so in order to dry my face I just relied on #14, on the list of *Things That Bandannas Can Be Used For*.

Primed and ready to start filming, my cameraman asked me what we should do first, so I went with my gut. "Just turn the camera on, follow me wherever I go, and let's see what happens." Which he did. The next two hours was nonstop, guerilla-style filmmaking at its *MTV Sports* finest. We "bum rushed" (great 90s term) anyone and everyone on and off the field, fans in the stands—hell, even Los Angeles Dodgers manager Tommy Lasorda got in on the action. It was all about energy, pace, and fun, and the more people we got involved or the more crowded it got, the better it was. I fed off of the electricity of the people and I honestly don't know who was more excited, me or them.

When we finished filming for the day, I was thrilled about footage we'd captured, but part of me was unsure as well. We'd addressed all of the bullet points Patrick wanted us to address, but in a rather unconventional way. I recall asking my cameraman what he thought about the shoot and he said laughing, "It was awesome...I'm not sure if it's what Patrick wanted, but it was awesome!"

Considering the intimate and artistic way in which we shot the wrap-arounds with Bo Jackson, the direction in how we shot that day was basically the other end of the spectrum. Also, the first episode of *MTV Sports* hadn't even premiered yet, so we had no pulse as to what the audience would like. At the end of the day, we met up with Patrick, who was exhausted from the *Rock n' Jock* production, but he was obviously curious as to how our shoot went as well. I remember trying to hide the nerves in my voice when I told him, "Well Rick, you're either going to love it or you're going to fire me."

Almost a week had passed since the shoot. Patrick was back in New York, and I hadn't heard a word from him or anyone else who worked on the show for that matter. When he finally called, he asked if I had a minute to talk. It didn't seem good, but I could never tell with him, because his demeanor was always very calm and cool. "I saw the footage and I think I know what direction we're going to go with the show." I still couldn't read him, "I think from now on, we're just going to cut you loose and let you do what you do best, and then we'll take that footage and do what we do best with it. The stuff was great!"

You know, I've often been asked who was responsible for my career, and truthfully, it's almost an impossible question to answer. But if I had to pick one person, it would be Patrick Byrnes. He's an incredibly talented producer who put his own ass and job on the line, by taking a chance on a no-name production assistant to host his show. Then, checking his own ego at the door, he took another chance by letting me do what I did best—he let me be me. I will forever be indebted to him for that. Always pay it forward with positivity, because there's something beautiful and magical in taking a chance, to give someone a chance.

That entire process was a huge career learning lesson for me. So often, in any profession and/or in life for that matter, people hold onto the belief that if things aren't done their way, then they're being done the wrong way. The truth is, when you open yourself up to embracing the creativity and ideas of others, you're also allowing yourself to grow by embracing the true ideal of what the creative process is all about. Some of the greatest ideas you've ever had were probably inspired right after you'd just heard a really bad one. Always remember, the conception of an idea is inherently brilliant, even the "bad" ones.

WAIT... PEOPLE ARE ACTUALLY WATCHING THIS?

January 25, 1992, the pilot episode of *MTV Sports* premiered, and apparently more than just me and the crew were watching. In less than a month after it launched, we were airing in 72 countries and were one of MTV's top-rated shows worldwide. I obviously knew a lot of this was happening, but having never worked on a show before, it took a while for me to really absorb the magnitude of it. Maybe it was because I was still living in Los Angeles and the show was produced out of New York, so I really wasn't too involved in the day-to-day aspect of it. That being said, I do recall the first time the popularity of the show became extremely real for me.

Hot on the heels of the show's initial success, Volvo contacted us with the hopes of appealing to "younger, hipper" car buyers. Their idea, which in my eyes was a pretty amazing one, was to fly me 90 miles deep into the Arctic Circle to Kiruna, Sweden. There, they wanted me to test drive some of their newer models on an ice track, which, in turn, would be filmed for an episode of our show. It was episodes like this one that made me feel like I was in a 90s Mastercard commercial.

- Salary per episode—$400
- 3 pack of bandannas—$14
- Macy's silver hoop earrings (because they don't turn your ears green like the "gold")—$20
- Crash a brand new speeding Volvo off an ice track into snow drifts, pet reindeer, and drink vodka in an ice hotel (not necessarily in that order)—PRICELESS!

After leaving New York, our flight had an early-morning layover in Stockholm. I think it was around 5 a.m. I remember the airport was basically empty, with the exception of our crew. Fewer than 10 of us were strewn out across a few benches trying to kill the two hours before our connecting flight to Kiruna. Then almost out of nowhere, walking in our direction, were three, twenty-something-year-old guys with duffles and ski caps. I glanced toward them as they got closer, figuring they were probably on our flight. They slowed a bit then said something in our direction in a foreign language that reminded me of the Swedish Chef from *The Muppet Show*.

I turned to see what they wanted and they were just standing there smiling when one of them said, *"MTV Sports? MTV Sports,* yes?!" I responded with a thumbs up and a stunned, "Yep, *MTV Sports*." I was caught off guard a bit to see how excited these guys were and how much they loved our show. We talked and took photos on their disposable cameras (remember those), then as the icing on the proverbial cake, one of them had me sign a bandanna from his duffle. They politely thanked us and hustled off to make their flight, leaving me and the crew sitting there jet lagged and amazed. I remember trying to grasp the fact that we were on the other side of the planet and just happened to get approached at 5 a.m. by three random guys who knew our show.

In reality, I was really proud because we were just a group of friends who were having fun creating a show based around things that we liked. To know that people across the globe not only watched it, but also enjoyed it, was kind of mind blowing. For me, this was the beginning of the realization that there was a huge underground population of extreme sports enthusiasts, even larger than I had thought. They loved us, because with *MTV Sports* we created a platform that gave them a voice and allowed them to let the world know they existed. (You're welcome *X-Games* ... insert winky-face emoji here.) Yes, it was definitely an ego boost, but more than anything, I was overcome with gratitude for being in a position to be a part of the show as well as that underground movement.

After another month of the show airing, another thing in particular was becoming glaringly apparent ... I was broke. The transition from my production assistant salary of $300/week to $400/episode as host of the show was hitting me right in the pocket where I carried my money. I would have said wallet, but I couldn't afford one at the time. Plus, the money I was carrying was more like loose change, so it would've just fallen out of the wallet anyway. This problem stemmed from the fact that we were only slated to shoot 20 episodes for the first season. As much as my 23-year-old brain would have liked to think I could stretch that $8,000 out for the whole year, I was still going to land quite a bit below the ramen noodle line.

So, I started looking for bartending jobs with the hopes that wherever I landed they'd be flexible enough not to fire me when I had to leave for a shoot. I also made Patrick Byrnes well aware of my situation, on the off chance he'd give me a pity raise. A couple weeks later, he let me know that after going to bat for me regarding my salary, that the show was just not budgeted to give me a raise. I figured as much but also wasn't sure what to do next, since I still hadn't found a second job.

Then he let me know one thing he had discovered. The show was budgeted to carry another production assistant on staff. So on that day, Dan Cortese, host of *MTV Sports*, happily accepted the position to become the West Coast production assistant of *MTV Sports* and personal assistant to Dan Cortese. I booked my own flights, cars, hotels, location scouted, you name it. I didn't care, I looked at it as being a triple threat, host, production assistant, and personal assistant, and that extra $300/week moved me not only above the ramen noodle line but well into the realm of the occasional Stouffer's French Bread Pizza. Life was good!

INTERMISSION, AKA MTV SPORTS (A FEW RANDOM EPISODES)

During the early run of *MTV Sports*, we received many accolades and my job in particular had been referred to by many in the media as, "the greatest job in television." Truth is, it was a dream job, and if I could do it all over again, I would, without hesitation, dive head first into the extreme bliss that was *MTV Sports*. For those of you don't know or may have forgotten the show, here's a few random episodes off of the top of my head to give you a bite-sized sample of some of the fun we had and places where we left some positive energy.

Pamplona, Spain

I lived out one of my childhood dreams and got to see firsthand what Ernest Hemingway referred to as "furious energy" when I laced up my Nikes and took part in the running of the bulls. This legendary event has been a staple of Spanish culture since the fourteenth century, so going into the day we knew this episode would prove to be an epic one—thus, everything had to be right.

The traditional running of the bulls attire consists of a red neckerchief, white shirt, and red sash. Out of respect, I kept with the theme and just grunged it up a bit. White shirt with an appropriately placed giant red bullseye on the back, red neckerchief, red sash, and of course, the necessary headgear, my red bandanna.

While I was aware that a run took place daily for eight consecutive days, I was not aware that 99 percent of the people that run are utterly hammered. Imagine a town of wasted Daytona Beach Spring Breakers getting their drunk sunburnt asses run the hell over by 1,200-pound bulls, literally run over. Only instead of G-strings and Speedos, they're wearing white shirts covered with Sangria and vomit stains. Yes, these fine folks toss back Sangria all night long, until the race starts at 8 a.m., then they attempt to run/stagger with the bulls. Then post-race/survival, they proceed to pass out all over the town square, wake up around 6 p.m., rinse and repeat.

Regarding my run, we were covertly filming it for the show, because at the time, it was illegal to do so. I recall trying to be "super-relaxed guy" for the camera—that was, until the ground started shaking like a 5.0 earthquake. As the bulls rapidly closed their gap with the masses, the reality of the situation hit me harder than a Jåger-bomb for breakfast. The sound of the thundering herd mixed with the exuberant panic of the people

FIGURE 16.1 That is not a smile on my face, that's me attempting to hide the terror and tears from the camera.

made "super-relaxed guy" act more like "Super F-this, I'm running for my life guy" (Figure 16.1). At that point, it was every man for himself. I was less concerned with filming the show and more concerned with not taking a bull horn to the ass.

Although, the aforementioned horn-to-ass concern almost did occur. As the fortunate ones who still remained ran for our lives toward the finish line at the colosseum bull ring, a staggering drunk frat boy (probably from Duke) fell down in front of me, causing me to do the same and I immediately had my left shoulder crushed by a bull hoof. By "crushed" I mean slightly grazed, just enough to leave a bruise, but I found the adjective "crushed" helped build the drama once I got into the colosseum to film the close of the show.

New York City

I was one of the fortunate few who rode in the New York Rangers ticker tape parade through the streets of New York City after they ended their 54-year drought of winning a Stanley Cup.

Trust me, you haven't seen New York until you've seen it from the back of a convertible in a ticker tape parade. Actually, it should have been called a "just throw whatever the hell you want out of your windows" parade. We were filming in the midst of one and a half million exuberant New Yorkers who were lining the streets and hanging out of windows. Mixed in with the downpour of confetti, a few of my favorite items falling from the sky that day were beach balls, a pair of men's briefs, and the slice of pizza that landed on our trunk. The pizza was not only surprising to see but also quite delicious.

#NewYorkStyle #ILoveNewYork #DMmeIfYouWantYour-BriefsBack

Churchill Downs, Louisville, Kentucky

It was a rainy day at the 1994 Kentucky Derby, and 157,000 people with giant hats, southern drawls, and Mint Julep buzzes were acting like the rain was just God's way of washing away their sins.

I'd never experienced anything like this, not just the sheer magnitude of it, but the commitment to its traditions from all in attendance. The Kentucky Derby is one of the biggest parties on the planet, and not only did I get to indulge in the party and smoke a cigar with Dennis Hopper in between races but we got to film at the finish line (Figure 16.2).

That day was also the first and last time I've ever placed a bet on horses. With the cameras rolling, I went to the betting

FIGURE 16.2   This is how you do the Kentucky Derby!

window and decided to drop $50 on my horse of choice, a 10-1 thoroughbred named Go For Gin. Why Go For Gin? Because one, I lacked any sense of gambling prowess and two, I liked drinking Tanqueray gin at the time.

With the crowd fever pitched and screaming at the top of their lungs, the horses raced down the back straightaway toward the finish line. Wouldn't you know it, Go For Gin was in the damn lead. I was jumping up and down more than Richard Simmons at a Dolphin Shorts sale in West Hollywood. With the gambling gods looking down upon me on that wet Saturday afternoon in May, Go For Gin went on to win the Kentucky Derby and I won $500, which I happily spent on beer for the crew later that night.

In an odd side note, I have a Twitter follower who claims he started betting on horses after seeing that episode of the show. That said, I'd like to take this moment to apologize to his wife for any monies lost—for the monies won, feel free to Venmo me my 20 percent.

Talladega Superspeedway, Talladega, Alabama

The Winston 500. This was not only my initial introduction to the beautiful state of Alabama, but my baptism by Miller Lite and Skoal chewing tobacco into the world of NASCAR racing.

There ain't no red quite like crimson red, trust me, and that's coming from a guy who spent his four years of college in North Cackalacky. This 2.66 mile oval track covered 270 acres, which by the race's end seemed to have had 269 of those acres covered in beer cans. The guy who has the recycling contract for the track must be ballin'.

Thanks to the good folks at Team Penske, we were lucky enough to be shooting an episode in the pits with team owner Roger Penske, Hall of Fame driver Rusty Wallace, and their talented pit crew. Being able to witness what takes place behind the scenes during one of these races and how it's a complete team effort was truly an eye-opening experience for me.

In a WTF sidenote, that shoot also, oddly enough, led to myself, Rusty, and some friends a few years later vacationing together on a 138-foot private yacht along the Amalfi Coast in Italy. Yes, an odd fact, but a fact nonetheless, which lands at #2 on the list titled, "Name two guys you never thought would hang out together." Number one on the list would definitely have to be the time I was in Cabo doing shots of Mezcal with Olympic Gold medalist and figure skating god, Scott Hamilton.

By the way, to the person who left their camera on the table next to us while they went to the bathroom, we apologize for all those photos of "random junk."

Wrigley Field, Chicago

This was one of my most memorable shoots because prior to this, seeing a baseball game at the fabled Wrigley Field was a staple on my bucket list.

The crew and I were really excited and surprised because the Cubs had honored us by designating it *MTV Sports* Day and because of that, I had been asked to throw out the first pitch. One thing the Cubs P.R. team failed to mention to us was, it was also Tony G's Barbershop Day, Maury Schwartz Mortuary Day, and some random School-for-Kids-Who-Don't-Like-Going-to-School Day. Seriously, we were sharing our "day" with at least five other "days." Truth is, we didn't care, we actually thought it was pretty hilarious and intentionally played up the honor of our big day on camera.

I not only got to throw out the first pitch for the Cubs game, or at least one of them (Figure 16.3), we got to shoot for half an inning with Cubs Hall of Fame play-by-play announcer Harry Caray. For those of you who don't know Harry, he was a one-of-a-kind character and a larger-than-life icon in the broadcasting community. The other thing that was larger than life were the beers he would drink during the game. If Bud makes you wiser, then Harry was freakin' Yoda.

When it came time for us to shoot with him, I was ushered into his booth while the game was in progress. For some reason, Harry was under the impression that I had recently interviewed then-President Bill Clinton, which I had not. The closest I came to that was doing Tequila shots in 1996 with his brother Roger Clinton, at a bar a block away from the Republican Convention in San Diego (feel free to add that as #3 to the previously mentioned list). But I digress . . .

FIGURE 16.3   This was one of my favorite shows we ever filmed.

So what do you do when Harry Caray wants to share a Bud-weiser and talk Slick Willy? You sip your Bud, nod your head a lot, and talk Slick Willy. To this day, that was my first and last on-camera "political" conversation. He was generous, hilarious, and quite engaging, and thanks to Harry, to this day, I still have "political analyst" on my resume.

Dublin, Ireland

I knew people were really starting to take notice of us when Paramount Pictures contacted the show and wanted us to shoot with Mel Gibson from the set of *Braveheart*. No, it wasn't a sports-related movie, but we didn't care, it was a free trip to Ireland to shoot with Mel.

A few days later, I landed in Dublin at 11 a.m., 10 hours before my crew was set to arrive. The hotel concierge had a rather novel idea for me. He gave me a list of three bars and suggested I go on a pub crawl in my down time. When I asked him why he only wrote down three pubs, he smirked, and responded, "You won't make it out of the second one," and he was right. Playing darts and drinking Guiness all day while simultaneously trying to decipher the Irish brogue with five men whose combined age was roughly 950 deserves to be a book in itself.

The following day, when we got to the set, I was hustled through hair and makeup, so I'd look the part of a thirteenth-century Scotsman, just like everyone else in the film. The angle for the episode was to have me work with the stunt crew who choreographed the battle scenes, so that when we got our ten minutes with Mel, he could give me pointers on what I'd learned.

Mel wasn't just starring in this epic picture but directing it as well. His time needed to be used judiciously so when he finally arrived, he obviously wanted to know exactly what we were going to shoot. To break the ice, I told him, "We're going to film you beating the shit out of me with that wooden mallet over there." Mel apparently thought this was the greatest idea of all time, and without hesitation, commenced to beating the shit out of me with the wooden mallet. The blood packs attached to each end of the mallet seemed to amuse him to no end. It didn't matter that I was

FIGURE 16.4   Not sure what hurt worse, the morning after the pub crawl or getting pummeled by Mel!

dizzy or that my ears were ringing, Mel was having fun pummeling away, and because of that, I knew this was going to make for a great episode (Figure 16.4). I still think the follow-up episode should have been shot during my CAT scan, but you can't always get what you want.

When our time with Mel was up, he looked at my bloodied face, laughed, and said, "Do you want to be in the movie?" Cut to the scene where Mel's character, William Wallace was being knighted: I was one of a group of Scottish clansmen *waaaay* in the back of the room. I was positive I wasn't on camera and my crew was simultaneously filming for our show, so I was making dumbass faces and dancing for our cameras. After the scene ended, Mel asked his cameraman how the shot looked and he said, "Great, except the asshole way in the back was dancing throughout it." Thus abruptly ended my chances at an Academy Award for my cameo in *Braveheart*.

A WHOPPER OF A DEAL

The popularity of *MTV Sports* felt like it was growing exponentially by the day. The media had a schoolgirl–like crush on the show because it was unlike anything that had preceded it, not just with what we covered but how masterfully it was edited and pieced together by our staff. If the huge following of the MTV generation wasn't proof enough of our success, the fact that we won MTV its first-ever Emmy Award and added another one to its mantel a year later was. We were not only changing the way people viewed sports but we were influencing how mainstream sports started shooting their programs as well. We opened the door to this fun, freewheeling visual approach, and mainstream sports followed us through it.

The media was also obsessed with this new, no-name guy hosting the show. Who is this guy? Cortez? Corteez? Where'd he come from? Why is he talking to the camera? What's with the bandanna? Was I what they call in Hollywood a "flavor of the month"? Initially, of course, I was—it's how the industry format works for newbies, build them up to tear them down. Always has been, always will.

The media requests for interviews and appearances were becoming increasingly more difficult for me to keep up with, but they were never burdensome. I was living my dream, so none of this felt like work, it felt more like the plain and simple fun that it was meant to be. It was because of the fun and popularity that money, or the lack thereof, stayed in the back of my mind.

That was, until the summer of 1992. We were in Hawaii filming an episode of *MTV Sports* and I received a call from my manager, who prefaced the conversation by telling me to "sit down." Apparently, he'd received a call regarding an offer for me, an offer unlike any we'd seen prior to this point. No, it wasn't an interview request or a mall appearance. This was, as they say, when "shit got real" in my professional career.

Burger King was launching a $150 million ad campaign called BK Tee Vee, and they wanted to feature me in the commercial spots. Dan Cortese as part of a $150 million ad campaign? Never in my wildest dreams could I ever fathom hearing that. They were also going to make an offer to my friend, Patrick Byrnes, to direct the commercials, which were to be shot in the same fast-paced, improv-driven vein as *MTV Sports*. That was followed by how much they were willing to pay me. Now remember, I'm the guy who was excited to make $11 an hour working the graveyard shift at a steel mill, a guy who still thinks $20 is a lot of money.

But, the executives at Burger King and their ad agency obviously had done their homework. They knew I was a 24-year-old kid who, that year, was set to make less than $20K for hosting my show, so what better way to get me on board than to hire my best friend then hit me right between the eyes with a bunch of zeros to get me to say yes. At that point in my career, it was definitely life changing money, so of course I was going to bungee jump right into the gig. Plus, I looked at it as a potential positive career move as far as increased visibility to non-MTV viewers. Little did I know that this deal would be an incredible learning lesson for me as to how the business works.

After a few weeks, with our negotiations almost completed we received a call from the MTV business affairs office in New York. The gist of that call was curt and to the point: Contractually, MTV had the right to approve or disapprove any on-camera jobs I was offered outside of the network. So, after internal discussions, MTV was refusing to allow me to take part in the BK Tee Vee campaign. I always laugh looking back at the fact that they were said to have had "internal discussions," because I'm sure that it was less of a discussion and more of a statement that sounded something like "Hell no he can't do them!"

Talk about a shot to the chicken nuggets. The network's message was loud and clear. We found you, you're our property, you will do what we tell you to do. Remember, I was less than six months into this hosting thing. I not only had no money, I also had no attorney...another lesson learned. Luckily, what I did have was access to *MTV Sports* t-shirts and a friend, who had a friend who was a lawyer.

It's weird how sometimes the most seemingly difficult situations can be addressed in the simplest of ways. Another lesson learned—don't overthink things. I didn't, basically because I was too young and too new to all of this. Also, I was alone and living

2,500 miles away from my family, so it was all on me. The rest of it went down like this: My friend's lawyer buddy wanted to meet me for drinks and said that if I gave him two autographed *MTV Sports* shirts, he'd look over my contract pro bono. That was a no brainer. I even brought two MTV baseball hats for good measure, then with a nervous Frank Burns–like giggle, I picked up the tab and prayed that my card wouldn't get declined in front of him. As silly as it sounds, at the time I felt this meeting was my only hope of keeping the deal alive.

Two days later, I received a "good news/bad news" call from the attorney, and like they always do in the movies, I went with the bad news first. That news was as follows. He said no matter how many years I worked at MTV, I would never make more than $400 an episode. He quickly followed that with a "more importantly, my *MTV Sports* shirt is fitting a little snug." After agreeing to send him a double XL, he asked if I'd like to meet to have beers again to make the swap. I assumed his small talk either meant the "good news" wasn't very good or he just wanted an excuse to get out of the house again.

After I agreed, he dove into the "good news." He happily told me that my contract had three paragraphs that were illegal under New York state law. I wasn't necessarily clear how that news was good, so he explained that if I kept my existing contract the way it was, I was free to do any other work I pleased without having to gain the network's permission. "Legally they can't hold you to it because it's an illegal deal. So keep cashing those $400 checks from here on out, and go make as much money as you can doing whatever you want on the side. So, how's about tomorrow at 5 p.m. for happy hour at Shooters?"

Just like that, the crisis was averted, and over the next five years of hosting *MTV Sports* my contract never changed. Once again, the power of the MTV t-shirt prevailed. Truth be told, even though the network was not pleased, I never harbored any ill will toward them. I'll always love MTV because I made lifelong friends there and was fortunate enough to be a part of something special that took place during the most influential time of the network's history. I've always looked at the contract issues as nothing more than my introduction into the business side of a creative industry.

So with the contract issues in the rearview mirror, I was happily crowned and set to become the face of BK Tee Vee. The plan was to film the commercials with actual patrons at Burger King's all over the country, with the hopes to really connect with their consumers. Initially it started extremely well, but then in an effort to save money, the ad agency fired Patrick, had its own executives direct the spots, and started scripting them as well. That's where we got more than a little off track. Let's just say, people on their lunch breaks in places like Harlem weren't too overjoyed when some guy with a backward baseball cap and camera crew would jump into their booth and say something like, "How's that whopper tasting, big man? Bet you wished you had a side of popcorn to go with that. Boom! Ask and you shall receive!"

The goal was to saturate the market with these spots, and saturate they did. We shot close to 100 commercials in total, I believe 15 to 20 were national spots and the rest were regional. They were everywhere. You couldn't switch the channel without seeing one. But as it always goes, if you have too much of something, you might not want it anymore. The media chose to turn up the flame-broiled heat on me. From David Spade on *Saturday Night Live* to David Letterman, I became the butt of some pretty hilarious jokes. Others also took a few cheap shots, but they were unintelligent attempts and basic at best, usually based around calling me a "sellout."

I remember being asked in an interview not too long ago that if I knew the way that the BK campaign would change a lot of people's perception of me, would I still have chosen to be a part of it? That's a simple answer, of course I would have. That job put food on my table, bought me my first house, and put money in the bank for the children I'd hoped to have one day.

Truth is, I've never really cared what others have thought about me, and I still don't. It's a waste of time and energy. I've always believed that internal strength is the foundation for external happiness. While some may have chosen to perceive me in a particularly negative way, that's fine, that's their choice. That became an unforeseen precursor for me dealing with the likes of today's social media trolls.

I've taken a simpler approach. I've chosen to believe in myself and strived to achieve my goals. The truth is, BK Tee Vee opened many more doors for me than it closed. Actually, it's too bad that deal didn't happen in today's media market. It would have been hard to label me a sellout for doing fast-food commercials when you've got Oscar winners hosting game shows. Oh well, to each his own. I hope everyone eventually gets their own whopper of a deal.

18

FLUFF YOUR LiPS AND THRUST THOSE HiPS

On a beautiful New York City night in the early 90s, I found myself gliding down the electric streets of Manhattan walking like I was a mashup of Tony Manero and George Jefferson. I didn't care, I was in New York, the only city I've ever been in where the energy enters the soles of your feet and almost as if a disco ball was hanging from your heart, visibly exits out of every pore of your being.

I was in town to spread my wings, grow my brand, and attempt to do something I'd never done before, be a model. I mean why not, it was the 90s, the decade that birthed the "supermodel." There were the likes of Cindy, Naomi, and Kate, why not add Dan into that mix? Although that's lacking the necessary *je ne sais quoi*, it probably only would have worked if I added an accent to my name and pronounced it "Day-on." There we go, much better.

The following morning I had an early call time for my shoot in SoHo, and just shooting there made me feel so-ho much like a model. I was excited, nervous, and truthfully, a little hungry... okay, a lot hungry. I remember being told by someone, or more than likely, it was my own brain, which came up with the concept to not eat dinner the night prior to, or breakfast the morning of the shoot, with the hopes of making myself look a bit more svelte.

This was a serious gig, so I stuck to my male modeling guidelines. It was an ad for Iceberg clothing, which was to be used in magazines and billboards in the US and Europe and was to be shot by world-renowned fashion photographer Steven Meisel. He was, and still is, one of the biggest names in fashion photography history. Not only had he worked with every top model of the day, he was fresh off of shooting Madonna's book *Sex*. So all of that being said and having never done anything close to this before, I seriously had no freaking clue what to expect.

I remember the car dropping me off outside of what appeared to be an abandoned warehouse, and the ground was shaking from the bass of the house music pouring through the cracks in the walls. Knowing all that I thought I knew about the fashion industry, I wisely deduced that I must be in the right place. Once inside the massive space, I didn't see a soul, just a lit set, a huge fan on each side of it, a rack of clothes, and the most incredible table of food packed with tempting spread of goodies for the non-svelte model types.

A few people started to emerge as I busted a move toward a bagel the size of a pizza. I quickly turned my bagel-diving reach into a handshake just in time to be greeted by a woman who whisked me off to a makeup chair for some much-needed help for my face. After I was pancaked and powdered, I was led to the wardrobe rack to choose an outfit for the shoot. Apparently, in the fashion industry, you don't need a private room to change clothes, all you need is blaring house music to divert attention away from your goods and grumbling svelte stomach.

Once I was hooked up and ready to go in Iceberg's finest, I was pointed to my mark in front of the lights, and within seconds of me reaching it, both of the massive fans turned on and almost blew me to Hoboken. I just stood there trying to clear the dust from my eyes, not sure if this was a photoshoot or an off, off Broadway production of *Twister*.

Then almost as if Scotty beamed him up, through my blurred vision I saw a figure appear with long black hair, a black beret, and a camera. He immediately started taking photos and yelling things in my vicinity and by that I surmised this must be Steven Meisel and that the shoot had begun. I was having trouble making out his instructions over the thumping music and howling wind in my ears, so I went to some of my predetermined go to moves, i.e., JCPenney catalog modeling poses I practiced in my hotel room that morning in front of a mirror. At one point, I recall him pausing, dropping the camera away from his eye and yelling something that I was having trouble deciphering. I believe our exchange went as follows:

   Steven: (Yells something inaudible)
      Me: What?!
   Steven: (Yells something more adamantly, but still inaudible)
      Me: What?!
   Steven: (Something that sounded like) FLUFF! YOUR!
           LIPS!
      Me: Fluff my lips?

Steven nodded his head, then bit down on his lips and I, quickly becoming quite the model, followed his lead and "fluffed my lips." He yelled what appeared to be, some sort of approval and then started rattling off photos to the reverberating beat of the music. I was caught up in the moment and was in what many models might call, "The Zone." Actually, I don't think any models call it that, but whatever it's called, I was there. With my lips more fluffed than a Four Seasons pillow, I began proudly ripping off some of the greatest pouty, duck-face poses 25 years prior to their birth on Instagram.

FIGURE 18.1 I believe this was JCPenney catalog pose #7 aka "The simultaneous tuck/untuck." Not an easy maneuver to pull off for a newbie.
ICEBERG ad campaign (1994; photographer: Steven Meisel)

Then almost as quickly as he appeared, Steven Meisel disappeared, leaving me and my lips alone on the set, wondering if I made him proud and oddly enough questioning the meaning of the lyrics to the now-thumping "You Spin Me Right Round" by Dead Or Alive. Then, reminiscent to when recess ends in grade school, the fans shut off and the same woman who greeted me approached me and said, "great job" and began to walk me out. Thankfully, she didn't notice my Copperfield-esque sleight of hand, as I slid a bagel in my back pocket right before I reached the door. Just like that, my dreams of high-fashion fortune and fame were over (Figure 18.1)—or were they? My meeting later that evening at Calvin Klein might have a say so in how this story ends.

BOXERS, BRIEFS, or BIRTHDAY SUIT?

Hot on the heels of the Iceberg shoot, I was ready to cash in on high fashion. A few hours later, I met with friends in Little Italy for a much-needed non-svelte Italian meal. After devouring a pound of pasta and a half a pitcher of house red, I was game ready for my meeting at Calvin Klein. I was given my marching orders via my manager in Los Angeles, and all I knew of the meeting were two things. One, "Calvin Klein and his people" wanted to meet with me, and two, they were looking for a new face or...well, let's just stick with face for right now, for their men's underwear line. Seemed easy enough, after I showered, changed and put on some CK cologne, that's right, I was always one step ahead. I made my way to their headquarters to meet **THE** Calvin Klein and show my sweet-smelling, showered face to him and a few other good people there.

The meeting was unlike any other I'd experienced to this point in my life. A crisp, New York autumn night had fallen over the skyline of the city by the time I arrived. Once inside, I was warmly greeted in the lobby by someone's assistant. He could have been Calvin's assistant or for all I know, he could have been Andy's in accounting, I had no clue, but he knew who I was so I followed him upstairs to a waiting room that looked like what you would expect a waiting room to look like at Calvin Klein headquarters.

It was just a bit odd to me that there was no one else around. Maybe this is how the whole fashion industry worked—people only appeared when necessary. And apparently two minutes later, it once again became necessary, as the same assistant came back into the waiting room to let me know that "they" were ready for me. Not sure who "they" were and/or if I should be doing something to get "ready" as well, but before I could make any type of annoying prerequisite small talk, the power-walking assistant had reached a nondescript door and pointed me inside.

There I was greeted by two women who were standing in front of a rather large rack of what I would soon find out to be different styles of Calvin Klein underwear. The rack was situated in front of a massive room divider with Asian designs on it. The two women were very polite and much better at the prerequisite small talk than the assistant. After a few random questions about my hair and nationality, one of them looked me up and down, pulled a pair of basic black briefs from the rack and said, "Here, why don't you put these on, they'll want to see them first." Then they turned to each other and started talking in a way that basically let me know they weren't planning on leaving the undie zone.

So, I slowly started to undress out of my best 90s grunge-era attire to gauge the privacy etiquette. I intentionally dropped the flannel that was strategically tied around my waist to the floor just to see if it would prompt them to exit, it didn't. So with that point taken, I proceeded to pile up my Pearl Jam wanna-be wear on the floor and changed into the skintight black briefs I was given. Seriously, if I would have applied them with super glue they would have been looser.

I stood there for a second, not sure what to do next, so I gave the courtesy clearing of the throat to let them know I was finished. The women turned and gave me a few surprised looks as if they hadn't even realized I'd been changing. Then one of them asked me if I was "ready." Maybe this was the "ready" the assistant was talking about and if it was, I knew I wasn't.

She led me and my barely there black briefs out from behind the room divider. I was shocked to find that on the other side of it was a massive office with roughly 10 people situated on a large couch and chairs quizzically staring in my direction. After an awkward pause the woman presented me to the crowd with a rather monotoned rendition of "Dan Cortese."

The people just looked at me in my underwear and I looked at them in their clothes wondering if I should be imagining them in their underwear. It worked for Jan Brady, so it was worth a shot. Unfortunately, all I was able to muster was a "What's up?" and I'm pretty sure my nerves caused me to swallow the "up," so it probably sounded more like "whassuh."

With that, someone from the couch said "Turn around, please." I did as I was told, and as I looked toward the back of the room I remember hearing the rather audible sound of the pasta I inhaled for lunch rapidly making its way through my intestines. The same voice from the couch then said, "Thank you," and the woman who announced me, quickly walked me back behind the divider.

This process repeated itself two more times, only with different styles and colors of underwear. To this day, I still have no idea if Calvin was even on the couch, or even Andy from accounting, for that matter. Needless to say, I didn't get the gig, but I was able to snag two pair of boxer briefs from the rack before I left, thanks to the fact that the two women didn't feel it was as necessary to watch me get dressed as it was to watch me undress.

Later that night, I was lying on the bed in my hotel room reflecting on my first day in the "fashion industry." I came to the conclusion that as bizarre as the day may have seemed to me, I was grateful for it having happened. No matter how much of my circulation was restricted by the black briefs or how much of it was increased by my fluffed my lips, I was thankful for the opportunity. It was the type of day not too many people ever have a chance to experience. Plus, in my mind, free bagels and boxer briefs easily label any day as a success.

YOU'RE JUST NOT DAN CORTESE, ENOUGH!

Having been blessed enough to work in the industry I love for over 25 years, I've come to learn many things about it. One of them being the fact that people in the entertainment industry are constantly being encouraged to reinvent themselves. I understand the reasoning behind this concept but also find the need for people to be very careful when attempting to do so. Because the truth is, the more people try to "reinvent" themselves, the greater the risk becomes of getting further away from who they really are. This problem can become an even more compounded issue when you're not sure who you really are to begin with.

I remember getting a call from my manager one day about a "slam dunk" commercial opportunity. Apparently, Gatorade was rolling out a new ad campaign, and the description for the attitude and voice of the commercials, read as follows: "The voice prototype for this campaign is Dan Cortese or a Dan Cortese–type." Well hello, with that my manager opened his Motorola flip phone, placed a call to the casting people in charge of the campaign and let them know that not only could they get a "Dan Cortese–type," they could get Dan Cortese. The only thing that closed quicker than his flip phone was the deal. All I had to do was go in for a voiceover session and just be me.

The script was pretty straightforward and so was the direction I was given by the producer. "Bring a lot of energy to it, but bring even more Dan, because that's what we want!" So, I did what I was told. Not only did I bring a lot of Dan, I even left some for them to nibble on after I was gone. The session was over relatively quickly. Not only was I pleased with how it went, but this had all the makings of the easiest job of all time. High fives and handshakes all around, and as I headed out, I even got a wink, a thumbs-up, and a lip-synced "nailed it" from the tech in the recording booth.

On the way home, my manager called me to see how the session went. I expressed my excitement about what had transpired, making sure not to leave out the thumbs up and lip-synced "nailed it" part just as a little added extra proof that he should really be proud of his client. He listened intently, then I could hear him take a long drag off of his Marlboro Light before saying, "Yeah, it's not going any further. You didn't get the gig."

In the midst of me trying to figure out if he was joking or not, he took another long drag and exhaled. I could almost hear the smoke staining the bonding on his teeth. "They said you did a nice job, but you weren't *Dan* enough, and that's specifically what they wanted." I wasn't Dan enough. As simple as that comment was, it sent me reeling a bit wondering what exactly WAS "Dan enough." I mean, for the love of God, I got a thumbs up and a lip-synced "nailed it," that led me to believe there had to be a good amount of "Dan" in that audition.

The truth is, that day and that comment sent my mind and career into a slightly different direction for a while. Whether it was consciously or subconsciously, when it came to work or work-related outings, I found myself always trying to give people more "Dan." It didn't matter if it was an audition, a meeting, or even making an appearance as a guest on a talk show. I would always be respectful to people working there, but at the same time, I'd give off as much of an IDGAF attitude as possible. Because that's who I thought people thought "Dan" was—that was the "Dan" they wanted.

When I shot new episodes for *MTV Sports* I felt the need to be bigger, more extreme, more in your face, more "Dan," I guess. I even found myself going into full on "Dan mode" when I'd meet people who were fans of mine. I truly thought that's what people wanted, that was the "Dan" they wanted to hang out with. Looking back now, I wish someone would have grabbed me by my bandanna and said, "Hey bud, let's bring it down a notch."

A few weeks later, I remember my manager giddily letting me know that he got a call from the good folks at Disney and that Jeffrey Katzenberg had requested to meet with me. Yep, that Jeffrey Katzenberg, not Geoff Kazenburg, the plumber from Poughkeepsie. At the time, he was well known across the globe as the chairman of Walt Disney Studios and I was known as the chairman of being "more Dan." So the fact that he wanted to meet me was not only a huge ego boost but something I viewed as a major career opportunity.

The meeting was set up as a breakfast at the Four Seasons in Beverly Hills. I would have been happy with the IHOP in Hollywood, but to each his own. I met my manager in the lobby and we were instructed to make our way into the lounge area outside of the dining room and wait there. As we made our way in, I remember walking with the proud purpose of a man who was about to have a meeting with Jeffrey *freakin'* Katzenberg. Once we got to the lounge, we were greeted by at least another five actors and their agents as well. They all had the same look of purpose that I did, but with every new guy who'd appear, it would diminish ever so slightly.

The truth was, we all had breakfast meetings with Jeffrey. Initially, I thought, "Damn, poor Jeff must have some sort of eating disorder." Then I came to realize that he was the man, and this was how he chose to do business. It was almost like speed dating except with bagels and lox...and with one of the most powerful men in Hollywood.

Each one of us got 10 minutes with him and the hopes of having him buy into whatever we were selling. When I was called in, my manager accompanied me, and the last thing I remember him saying to me was, "Just be you, be Dan." I would have rather he said, "Good luck," or even, "Don't suck," but either way, the seed was planted.

The meeting was going really well and I felt like we were getting along quite nicely in a Disney sort of way. I was just being me. Then Jeffrey asked me a question along the lines of how I was hoping to change people's lives with my talents and almost as if someone pulled the windup string on my back, I attempted to be "more Dan." Without thinking I remember starting my response with, "Let's be honest, in the intergalactic scheme of things, I'm not curing any diseases, I just want to entertain people." I followed that up with some more verbal diarrhea that my brain has wisely chosen to courtesy flush from itself.

When I finished, I remember feeling quite proud that I had displayed just the right amount of "Dan." After a brief pause, Jeffrey looked at me, smiled, and said, "Well, that's where you and

I see things a little differently." He proceeded to tell me stories of many successful projects he'd helped to create, like *Lion King*, and not only the financial success they'd had but the differences they had made in people's lives. Now some of you reading this may consider that a bit obnoxious, but when you're stating facts, it's just called the truth.

The meeting came to an end shortly after. I stood and shook Jeffrey's hand and thanked him for his time. He looked at me and said, "Good luck with everything" Now if you Google translate that from executive speak to layman's terms, it translates to, "Hey bud, next time bring it down a notch." Point taken, and two lessons learned:

1. Don't be the person that you think people want you to be, be the person that you know you are. That's a lot easier said than done, but a very smart man once told me, a good place to start is to truly not give a shit as to what others think of you, then go and grow from there.

2. No matter what business you're in, are you in it just to be in it, are you in it to just make money, or are you in it to make a difference? Do the best that you can to be a positive difference maker.

21

MORE DAN, BUT LESS MELROSE, I SUPPOSE

The line between work and reality is a very fine one for actors, or anyone in the public eye, for that matter. As I referenced in the prior chapter, over a period of time, it became a bit difficult for me to just "be me." Whether I was at work or in public, I found myself searching for an acceptable portrayal of "Dan" that would please others, but not necessarily myself. This issue can become even more convoluted when people associate you with a character you've played instead of you, the person who portrayed said character.

I was fortunate enough early on in my career to have the opportunity to audition for Hollywood legend and producer extraordinaire, Aaron Spelling. He'd created numerous hit shows over the prior three decades and, at the time, was riding another massive wave of success thanks to two new creations of his, *Beverly Hills 90210* and *Melrose Place*. I was asked to come in and audition for a new character on *Melrose Place*, Jess Hanson. He was the long-lost, evil half-brother of Jake Hanson, played by the talented Grant Show. The character of Jess was to appear in the last nine episodes of the season. Now, at that point in my life I'd never seen an episode of *Melrose Place*, but I obviously knew that this was one of the most popular shows on television, if for no other reason than its rabid adorning fan base.

A day before the audition, I was told by my stereotypically fast-talking, eye-twitching, never-trusted-him, if Ari-Gold-and-Spongebob-had-a-kid-it-would-be-him agent, that Aaron would not hire any male leads if they had long hair and/or facial hair. At the time I had both, and therefore I not only had a minor career dilemma hanging over my hairy head but I also had a decision to make. It seems like a no brainer and is simple to just say, "Cut the hair and shave, Dan. Just think of the money you'll save on conditioner." But in my mind, I believed that "look" added to the sinister mystique of the character and in keeping it, would hopefully separate me from the other guys auditioning. (How's that for some stereotypical, b.s., Hollywood rationale for you?) Plus, I also felt it may have been a ploy by Agent Spongebob to get me to do what he'd been wanting me to do for a while, which was to "cut that shit." So, I decided to do what any other intelligent actor would do in my situation. I ran lines while looking at myself in the mirror. And after checking my good side twice, I decided to "keep my shit."

When I arrived for the audition the following day, I remember seeing all the clean-cut actor faces there competing for the same job as me. Every one of those guys looked like they could star in an Aaron Spelling show, whereas I looked like a roadie for a band who would be opening up for Toad the Wet Sprocket in Columbus, Ohio. Just as I realized that my decision might not have been the wisest, my name was called to go in and read. This was it, I had no other alternative than to do my best to bring Jess Hanson to life in that room.

When I walked through the door, I immediately saw that there were about six or seven people in the audition room and Aaron was sitting front and center on a couch. Thankfully, this time I wasn't in my underwear, although it would have been a pretty bizarre plot twist if Calvin Klein was sitting next to him. Anyway, I was greeted with a warm welcome from everyone, I responded by taking a chair from the back of the room and moving it about two feet in front of Aaron. From there I let the hair and goatee work for me as I did my best to take this asshole-of-a-character, off the page and introduce him in person.

Truthfully I knew I wouldn't get the job, so my goal was to attempt to just scare the shit out of everyone in that room. You know, kind of like in the original *Rocky*, when he knew he couldn't beat Apollo, so he just wanted to go the distance with him? (I think that just got me another slice from Mike's Place.) When I finished my audition, the only thing I remember was a deafening silence. Not sure if it was a "Wow, what a great job!" silence or a "Please leave now or we're calling security and a barber," silence. So, I returned the chair to its original position, thanked everyone in the room for the opportunity, and abruptly exited.

Later that night, I got a call from my agent, and all I really remember about it was some random squealing, followed by, "I gave him your number and he's going to call you any second." No sooner he spewed that out, my call-waiting alerted me of someone on the other line. Proof again that I was ballin' at this point in my career, I had the call-waiting. I quickly answered it and someone said, "Is this Dan?" I confirmed it was, then the voice said, "Hold for Mr. Spelling." Hold I did, mainly my breath. I mean, it's one thing to audition for an icon but it's another thing to have an actual conversation with him.

When Aaron got on the line, he did the majority of the talking, mainly because he was the one who called, and thanks to my nerves I stayed silent. I didn't want to accidentally throw out anything like, "How 'bout them Dodgers, huh?" Fortunately, not only was Aaron extremely talented, but he was also very kind as well. He complimented me on the audition, of which two things he said stuck out: "I loved the look," and, "You really scared the heck out of me." I was really hoping for "shit" but "heck" works just fine under these circumstances, too. He ended the brief, very-much-appreciated call with a congratulatory, "Looking forward to see what you do next week on set." Yo, Adrian, not only did I go the distance, but I got the decision!

The following week I excitedly arrived on the *Melrose* set for my first day of filming. I was quickly shown around, run through wardrobe, and then taken to the hair and makeup trailer. Once inside, I was greeted by my makeup artist, who introduced himself, then abruptly took out some clippers and turned them on. Almost as if in slow motion, he brought the clippers toward my face in the most Sweeney Todd of ways. When I asked what he intended on doing, he let me know that there was "no facial hair allowed on the show." With that, he proceeded to shave my entire face so smoothly that I looked like a porcelain doll that needed a nose job.

With my newfound face fresh and clean, I was taken out to set to shoot my first-ever scene for *Melrose Place*. The crew was as friendly as could be, and I even saw a few guys there who I'd worked with on other jobs. Being the new guy, that helped put me at ease a bit, but meeting the director immediately turned that ease to anxiety.

He greeted me with a reverberating rendition of "Oh my God! Why the hell did you shave?!" I did my best to explain what transpired earlier, to which he immediately escorted me back to the hair and makeup trailer by doing the "I'm walking really fast because I'm really pissed off" walk. Surprisingly, neither the makeup guy nor I were fired. But the faux pax led to me having to come in an hour earlier every morning for the next three weeks to get a fake goatee cut from a wig and glued to my face. A little skin toning side note, removing latex glue from your face for that long not only exfoliates your skin, it ex-freakin'-hurts it as well.

With that merkin-esque misstep a few months behind us, my run on the show was just about complete. We were closing in on the end of the season and were just about finished filming our cliffhanger finale episode. I won't lie, I truly enjoyed my time on *Melrose Place* playing this ruthless prick of a character. It was something exciting and new for me to sink my teeth into creatively.

The finale saw my character, Jess, propose to Daphne Zuniga's character, Jo, to which Jo said "no," and after she refused to let Jess force the ring on her finger, he decided to beat her up. Did you follow that? It was a soap opera after all; work with me, people. The controversial scene was brilliantly constructed and shot by our director, Charles Correll—actually, maybe too brilliantly.

About a week or so after FOX aired the highly rated finale, I was approached by two women on the street as I was leaving my favorite Mexican restaurant in Santa Monica. It's a little difficult to describe them, but I'll give it a shot. Imagine Boss Hog from the *Dukes Of Hazzard* in drag, you got that visual? She's the one who did all the talking. "Are you Jess Hanson?" As I began to explain, that was just the name of a character I played on the show, she showered me with more expletives than a drill sergeant getting hit in the balls during boot camp. I did my best to keep calm and remove myself from the situation, but she followed me down the street for a bit waving her finger like she was doing some sort of Harry Potter sorcerer shit.

When I finally turned back around, she looked at me and said, "How could you do that to Jo? She's such a sweet girl, why would you hit her?" "I didn't hit her!" "Yes, you did, I saw you!" I'd had enough of this woman at that point and rather flippantly I said, "I don't know, probably because they paid me to." To which Boss Hoggess promptly spit on me, said, "Rot in hell, asshole!" and stomped down the street to wait for the Star Tours bus. Looking back at the confrontation, it would have worked perfectly as a "deleted scene" for that season's DVD collection.

The conundrum I was left with from that day forward was this. How can I be more "Dan," less "Jess," more MTV, less Burger King, more extreme, less obnoxious, more engaging, less "in your face," but you know ... still be me, because that's what people want to see.

DRINKING WITH THE GENERAL

I briefly mentioned in the Introduction of the book, how blessed I was to have the opportunity to star in a CBS series with the legendary George C. Scott. Our friendship was one that many people easily responded to by saying, "What the hell would these two even have in common? I guess, George can talk about his Oscar and Dan can talk about...George's Oscar, too." The truth is, we had a helluva lot more in common than you'd think, although our evolution to get to that realization was not your typical one.

The series we starred in was called *Traps*, a one-hour cop drama shot in beautiful Vancouver, B.C. For those of you who don't know, the working hours on a one-hour series can be extremely long and demanding. Because of that, George had it in his contract that due to his age, health, and the fact that he was an Academy Award winner, he would work only eight hours a day and not one second more . . . literally.

As soon as the director would call action on the first shot of the day, George would reach down to his old-school Casio digital watch and start an eight-hour timer. It didn't matter if he was in the middle of the greatest take in Hollywood history, when that watch chirped to alert him the eight hours had passed, he would immediately, yet politely excuse himself with a "Good-night, everybody."

That was a great perk for George and deservedly so, he had earned it. It was not so much a perk for me on the other hand, especially since we were in almost every scene together. Because of it, we would only shoot master shots and George's coverage for every scene scheduled for the day. Once he left, we'd then have to go back to each scene and shoot my coverage. Therefore, I was constantly working overtime, 12- to 14-hour days, five days a week on *Traps* while still traveling to and from Vancouver on the weekends to squeeze in episodes of *MTV Sports* around the globe. This did wonders for my bank account, not so much for the inflatable-raft-sized bags under my eyes or my well being.

The longest span I went was 39 days without a day off. It became sort of a badge of honor for me, and quite frankly, I think it endeared me to George as well. He appreciated the fact that I appreciated and respected him and his body of work enough not to be an ass about it and/or to rock the eight-hour boat.

Honestly, I was never upset about it, I'd wake up every morning and think "Holy shit, I get to work with George C. Scott today." It still blows my mind to think that I'd be on set and get the occasional morning knock on my trailer door, only to find George standing there saying, "You want to run lines, Serpico?"

At the end of that 39-day stretch, day 40 was a rainy Sunday in the 'Couv and rather than sleep, I chose to go to the hotel bar, eat pizza, drink some beers, and watch football. It was a dark, mid-afternoon, and the only people there were myself and the bartender, so I decided to call my friend. To this day, I'm not sure what really compelled me to do so, probably the higher alcohol content in those damn Canadian beers. But truthfully, I didn't know anyone else in town and I was a bit lonely.

The bartender handed me the house phone and asked who I was calling, I responded with "A buddy of mine who I work with." I dialed George's room and as the line was ringing, I remember thinking, "Maybe this isn't the best idea, we've never hung out other than at work. What if he's asleep? What if I piss him off?" You know, lame excuse kind of stuff like that. As my mind was racing, he answered the phone:

> "Yeah?"
>
> "Hey George, it's Dan."
>
> "Yeah?"
>
> "I was just calling to see what you're up to?"
>
> "I'm on the can, Darling!"
>
> "Oh damn, I'm sorry! I'm just down at the bar and wanted to see if you wanted to have a drink? But, if you're busy..."

(I waited for him to interrupt with a response, but to no avail. Then after a long pause that almost prompted me to say "hello?" he replied.)

"I'll be down when I'm finished."

"Okay great . . . so about how long?"

(To this day still not sure why I asked that. Probably my nerves trying to fill the silence.)

"Could be two minutes, could be two
hours, whenever I'm finished!"

(George hangs up.)

Cut to 20 minutes later. I was considering leaving, thinking he wasn't going to show, but I was afraid to just in case he did make an appearance and I wasn't there. So basically, I knew I had to hunker down at the bar for good and wait it out one way or the other.

A few minutes later, the afternoon changed. From my vantage point at the end of the bar, I could see out the entrance, across the entire lobby and to the hotel elevator doors. Then almost as if in slow motion, the elevator doors opened and standing there alone was George C. Scott, looking as badass as you could possibly look in a hotel elevator.

He was wearing a robe and slippers, but not Sutton Place Hotels finest. He was wearing his own worn-for-years-probably-got-them-for-Christmas comfy plaid swag from home. People were double taking as he strolled across the lobby with his hands in his robe's front pockets and head held high.

I couldn't help but think, "He's the coolest son of a bitch on the planet," while simultaneously shitting my pants not knowing what to do once he sat down. Even the bartender was like, "Wait, that's your friend, eh?" Once George entered the bar I got up, hugged him, and offered him the seat next to mine. He smiled, looked at the accessories I happened to be wearing, and as he sat down and said, "Take those goddamn earrings out of your head, Nancy." And just like that, the ice was broken.

So what goes better with some broken ice than some cocktails. The bartender nervously inquired about George's order, to which he simply responded, "Glass of vodka, beer chaser." The rest of the volley went as follows:

> "On the rocks?"
> "No."
> "Chilled?"
> "No."

The bartender then filled what looked to be a double shot glass with Stoli and slid it in front of George, to which he responded with a look that led me to believe a "Patton slap" was going to make an appearance in the near future.

George then smiled and very poignantly again said, "I want a *glass* of vodka, beer chaser" at this point I felt the need to jump in and go all Wild West saloon and say, "Just leave the bottle and put it on my tab." Which the bartender promptly did, and our afternoon was off and running, as was my bartab. Holy alcohol markup, Batman!

My fears of potential awkwardness between us were all but gone after a few sips of Russia's finest and some genuine laughs. The rest of our afternoon turned into quite an unexpected, heartfelt, conversation, not just about work but about life. More often than not, on all of our journeys, it's those impromptu moments when there are no expectations of what will occur that turn into some of the most appreciated, memorable times of our lives.

As the afternoon turned into a rain-soaked evening, his unparalleled candor was on full display. When I asked him why he refused to accept his Academy Award, George chose to honestly answer the question that he'd answered a thousand times prior, as opposed to slapping my Nancy-assed earrings out of my head.

He took a swig, raised his voice a bit, then with the slightest hint of a laugh he said, "Because it's acting, Danny, it's not the Olympics. I didn't jump higher than everyone else or win a god-damn race, so why should I get an award for doing my job to the best of my ability?" He was chastised by many in the media for this opinion and for declining to accept the award. But whether people agreed with it or not, you had to respect the balls it took for him to tell Hollywood that about their most prized posses-sion. Plus, I've always felt, those who most vehemently opposed his view did so because deep down inside, they knew he was right. Acting is an art, and the beauty of art differs in every set of eyes that view it. So how can you truly say that some art is better than others? To do so is to state an opinion, not state a fact.

There was one thing from that day that made a huge impact on my life, and it's something that I will always embrace. It was the fact that of all the people on the planet, the first one to pro-fessionally appreciate me as an actor, above anything else, was George C. Scott. He didn't see me as the MTV guy or the Burger King guy, or any other guy, for that matter. He didn't care about any of that, he simply told me, "I appreciate you for what you are. A helluva good actor."

Now, while many of you may feel that I'm mentioning that to shine some positive light on my career, feel free to do so, but you'll be wrong. Because when I said George was the first person to appreciate me as an actor, I was including myself with those who didn't necessarily view me in that way. Hearing him say those words was the obvious kick in the ass that I needed to see myself in that same light. I needed to accept that it was okay for me to be proud of all the hard work I'd put in and that it was good for me to appreciate me. As I referenced in the very beginning of the book, if you don't like the narrative of your story, become the narrator. That seed was planted in my conversation with George that day.

As he began gathering himself to leave, he got up from his seat and tightened the belt on his robe. George said, "Don't ever give a damn what anyone else thinks, Danny. Because when you get caught up in all of that other bullshit, you lose sight of who you are."

With that, George downed the last bit of Stoli in his glass, then turned, and as he started to walk out of the bar, he yelled back without looking, "I'm going to sleep now, Darling. Don't call me anymore tonight." And just like that, George C. Scott walked out of the bar, across the lobby, and entered the elevator in the same manner as when he arrived an hour earlier. Head held high and not giving a damn what anyone else thought.

Nip, Tuck, and Liposuck!

Let's be honest, one of the most talked-about topics inside and outside of Hollywood is which celebrities have had work done. Then, of course, once we think we've unveiled who is having the work done, the next logical step is to decipher what exactly they've had done. Truthfully, back in the day it was much easier to figure out who had what done because you only had to deal with nose jobs, boob jobs, and facelifts.

Today the big three still exist, but now when you throw lip injections, liposuction, botox, fillers, chemical peels, and butt lifts into the mix, things can get a bit tricky. I prefer to keep it old school and just fluff my lips whenever the moment deems it necessary. Truth be told, at one time or another, everyone in Hollywood has had "something done," and yes, you can add me to that list.

One of the perks of working for MTV when I did was that I got to travel and see parts of the world I otherwise never would've seen. On a beautiful June afternoon in 1995, I found myself on Waikiki Beach in Hawaii shooting *Beach MTV* with my friend, Daisy Fuentes. Not only were we there to shoot for MTV, but we were also there to attend the star-studded opening of Planet Hollywood's newest restaurant. The things that took place at those openings could have had a six-part NC-17 Netflix documentary made about them alone. Gotta love the pre–social media 90s.

The way we shot *Beach MTV* was extremely freewheeling. The formula was basically this: Dan, do whatever the hell you want, just make sure to shut up right before Daisy says something like, "Dan you're stupid. Up next is *I Get Knocked Down* by Chumbawumba." On this particular day, we were shooting with some beachgoers at a lifeguard stand and I chose to use some props for the bit. So as Daisy started the segment, I went into a massive first-aid kit, pulled out a neck brace, and wore it for the remainder of the segment. When we finished what was maybe a minute and a half long bit, I was approached by two of our massive bodyguards, who were both native Hawaiians.

Suddenly things got pretty serious, I felt like I was in the episode of *The Brady Bunch* when Greg wore the tiki idol necklace and then busted his ass surfing. In a nutshell, they told me that wearing the neck brace when I didn't need it was not the wisest of choices due to the fact that it could invite some bad island mojo. I obviously didn't want to make the same mistake as Greg Brady, so I took off the neck brace, put it away and hopefully locked up any type of bad island mojo with it.

Later that night inside Planet Hollywood, there was a small group of celebrities who were in town for the opening the following night. Everyone was watching NBA playoff games and the pre-partying had already commenced. Daisy and I were a part of the group, as was our manager, who was in town for the festivities as well. Nature was calling, so I excused myself to go to the restroom, which was downstairs at the bottom of a massive escalator. My attire for the evening needs to be noted—a black tank top (because I'm Italian and at the time, I thought I was buff), ripped jeans that were about 2 inches too long, and flip flops.

As I got on the top of the escalator I quickly calibrated the speed it was traveling, with the long distance to the bottom of it, compared to how badly I had to go to the bathroom. My bladder then made the executive decision to pick up the pace a bit. So, I began to sort of skip down the escalator. As a side note, grown men should never skip . . . anywhere. My skipping, added to the fact that the escalator was still moving, combined with my too-long jeans clipping my flip flops, led me to not only lose my balance, but go stage diving toward the teeth near the bottom of the metal monster.

I recall getting my hands out in front of myself to break the fall, but again thanks to the escalator's ability to move its steps, this caused me to misjudge the timing as to when I felt the impact would occur. Therefore, my hands, which were supposed to break the fall, ended up by my side when the contact actually took place. Luckily my face was there to absorb the brunt of the fall, because only God knows where I'd be now if I would've cut up my hands instead.

After I landed, I remember immediately sitting up and literally saying "Fuck, I can't believe I just landed on my face." Then, in a blur, someone grabbed me under my arms and dragged me into the front of the kitchen and left me on the floor, and someone else quickly gave me a giant bag of ice to put on my face.

In hindsight, the kitchen was probably not the smartest place to take a profusely bleeding man, but I needed all the help I could get at that point and it was greatly appreciated. (Thankfully they already had their restaurant hygiene grade, it was an A. Pretty sure after this incident they were graded O+.) We've all seen how bad guys bleed when they cut their faces shaving, so you can only imagine how good I was looking. My blue jeans were now red jeans.

In the chaos taking place around me, I recall hearing my manager racing into the kitchen frantically asking where I was. Once he found me, I took the ice bag from my face and said, "How bad is it?" to which he responded with a shrieking "Call 911!" The next thing I knew, I was in an ambulance with paramedics, my manager, and a kind, older man who I assumed was a doctor due to the fact that he seemed to be sort of in charge from my blurred vantage point.

I don't really remember feeling any pain, but I do remember feeling oddly at ease. Maybe I was in shock, maybe the paramedics were the greatest actors ever, or maybe both. But I remember having an overwhelming feeling of calmness regarding my situation. This also may have been due to the fact that I hadn't seen myself in a mirror yet.

Just prior to our arrival at the Queens Medical Center hospital, there was a concern from my manager. He wanted to know if there would be a plastic surgeon on site to perform my surgery. I mean after all, I was a "mimbo" right? I kind of made my living with my face. Plus, it was approaching midnight on a Saturday night in Honolulu; it's not like plastic surgeons are just chillin' at the emergency room saying, "I might hang for another ten minutes or so just in case some dumb ass falls face-first down an escalator."

When we arrived, the older man in the ambulance let us know that a plastic surgeon, Dr. Benjamin Chu, would be meeting us there to perform the surgery. With my manager's fears somewhat put at ease, I was hurried into an operating room, where I was cleaned and prepped for surgery. It was at this point I begged to go to the restroom, having never had a chance to go before I ate a face-full of escalator grate.

I was allowed to go in the bathroom just off of the operating room and that was when I saw myself for the first time. It's hard to explain what went through my mind as I stood alone in that silent room. I vaguely recognized the person who was looking back at me, not sure if I wanted to cry or kick myself in the ass for bringing on the bad island mojo. With my nose broken both across the bridge and down the side, my left nostril detached from my nose, only hanging by where the skin met my cheek and a plethora of gashes above my lip, I figured I should probably get back in the operating room as soon as possible to hopefully have Dr. Chu put Humpty together again.

I couldn't tell you how long the operation took, but I kind of remember the doctor talking about working in Pennsylvania while he stitched my face as if he was embroidering a pillow that said "Happiness is...". After over 80 stitches were placed on both the inside and outside of my face, I do recall Dr. Chu telling me it was a good thing I had a big nose because it broke my fall and stopped me from crushing my cheekbones. Look at Chu with the jokes. Actually, I always believed there was probably some truth to that comment.

Then in the plot twist of the night, as Dr. Chu was leaving, I thanked him profusely and told him to also thank his friend, the older man from the ambulance for calling him. Dr. Chu then let me know he had no idea who the man was. He was just told that there was an emergency and that he needed to get to the hospital immediately. Later, we found out that the man wasn't a part of the paramedics medical team, either. They thought he was with my manager and me. So at this time I'd like to say, the only way to beat bad island mojo is with a good guardian angel. Or tell Ashton Kutcher that I need to see that lost episode of *Punk'd* where I break my face and The Hoff gets prosthetics, then goes all *Touched by an Angel* and saves the day.

Needless to say, I was not present at the Planet Hollywood Grand Opening the following night, although I'm pretty sure part of my DNA was still on the floor somewhere to represent me in spirit. Due to what was later explained to me as "some legal concerns," I heard from none of the good people of Planet Hollywood. The one and only call I got was from Danny Glover, who was also in town for the opening. He was the lone person to pick up the phone and not just check on my face but truly be concerned with how I was doing. Without going too much into detail, just know he's about as real as they come and a straight-up good human being. Which is a refreshing trait to see, not only in Hollywood, but anywhere in the world these days. Sometimes the smallest gestures are the ones that leave the largest impressions.

After basically hiding out in my house for six months waiting for all of the swelling to subside, I was finally able to have reconstructive surgery done for my nose and scaring. Thanks to another insanely talented plastic surgeon and one of the coolest people you'll ever meet, Dr. Harry Glassman I was able to get my face as close to Mimbo playing shape as possible.

After all these years have passed, I look back on that particular night and realize something. That fall that I took, one that many may consider such a negative experience, was actually quite the opposite. As I stood alone in a Queens Medical Center bathroom, looking in the mirror at my shredded face prior to my surgery, I was overcome with a sense of gratitude. I was grateful that the accident wasn't worse than it was and it was also the first time in my life that I realized the extreme importance of living

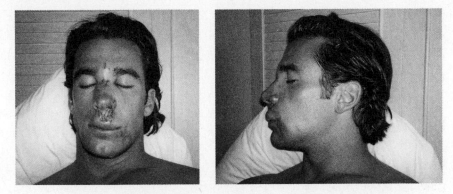

FIGURE 23.1 Escalator: 1, Dan: 0.

life in the moment. People like to say, "There's always tomorrow," but that's not necessarily true. One thing that is true is that there is always right now. So with that realization, I made sure I absorbed every single thing about that point in time as I looked in the mirror (Figure 23.1).

We hear "live in the moment" so often, but it's much easier said than done. Because to truly live in the moment, you have to be present for all of them, not just the good ones. But if you're able to do so, you can find beauty where you may have otherwise never thought it could exist.

The truth is, we've all "fallen down our own escalator" in life, some of us more often than others. It's not how we fall down that matters but how we get back up, how we learn, and how we move on. Live life, love life, appreciate life—one dream, one escalator, one moment at a time.

PART 3
FATHERHOOD

WHERE DA HOOD AT?

aving worked nonstop, 24/7 for the first 10 years of my career, I'd always tried to the best of my ability to recognize, appreciate, and use the lessons life had taught me to that point. I then attempted to use all of that knowledge and incorporate it into how I approached the rest of my life and work. So, I compiled everything in a giant manilla folder, labeled it **"Kinda Important Stuff You Might Want To Remember, Dan"** and stored it in the far reaches of my brain. I then would only bring it out when a situation deemed it necessary. Usually, those situations would occur right before I was about to royally screw up. It would act as a little tap on my shoulder, followed by my conscience saying, "You sure you want to do that, Big Man?"

Side by side with the lessons learned, I fondly think back to the freewheeling fun of traveling the world with MTV, the Rock n' Jock games, the days of Whopperfied flame-broiled funk, getting tipsy with George C., eating an escalator, and mimbo fever. Also, not to be forgotten were countless amazing experiences I shared with so many other fabulously talented people I've worked with over the years. Many have kindly asked me not to spill their secrets in this book. So spill I will not. I've cherished every moment of the glorious madness of my career, both the good and the not so good. I've truly been blessed and honored to have worked with and met some of the most talented people this industry has ever seen.

But all of that being said, none of those life lessons or experiences came close to preparing me for the greatest gig I've ever had…becoming a father. The truth is, the day you hold your child in your arms for the first time and they look into your eyes, your perception of the world and yourself, instantly changes forever. The day that occurred for me, I was no longer Dan, I was Dad, and ironically enough, I knew *exactly* who that was.

Unlike a lot of men, becoming a father had always been my biggest dream of all. So, for me to experience that dream not once, but three times, just triples the amount of immeasurable gratitude I have for my life.

But, for me to truly understand my journey as a father and continue to learn and get better at it, I have to look at when it started and where I've been. In doing so, I can hopefully see where I need to go, to continue to grow, as a father. The following are a few random "where I've been" parental moments that I've encountered along the way.

WILD CHILD DEVELOPMENT

As far back as I can remember, I've always wanted to be a father. Because I was quite verbal about this as a young high school student, I scared off many potential girlfriends...or it could have been the acne and all-pro spitting gap between my front teeth. Actually, nah, I'll go with the "wanting to be a dad" thing.

By the middle of my senior year of high school, the majority of my college requirements were fulfilled, but I needed a few random hours to fill out my schedule. So I chose an elective course I'd been wanting to take for quite some time. The class was called *Child Development*, which was a bit ironic because I'm not sure how much development actually took place in there. The course was basically a daycare that included toddlers of teachers in the school district who couldn't otherwise afford the help with their kids.

I was the only male student in the class, and I recall one or two of the girls in there being pregnant, so they probably took the course a bit more seriously than I did. Since I was the only guy, by default, I was in charge of all of the boys. For the record, I'm using the term "in charge" very loosely. The kids loved me because I genuinely enjoyed being with them and also because I loved me some "Duck, Duck, Goose." Every time we'd play it, I would play like it was game seven of the NBA finals. Thus, nine times out of ten, I'd get "goosed."

Another thing the kids were fond of was, whenever I'd be asked to take the boys to the bathroom for their "group pee," I'd always let them back away from the urinals and have a contest to see who could "go" the furthest. Having referenced that, now might be a good time to apologize to the Quaker Valley High School janitorial staff circa 1986. We cleaned up as best we could, but those bathroom paper towels weren't exactly the quicker picker upper. They were more like the slower smearer all overer.

I guess the reason I bring all this up is because I never got tired of that class and in fact, I always looked forward to it. In my 18-year-old mind, it was proof that I needed to have a child of my own, no matter how naïve that desire was at the time.

Unfortunately or fortunately, depending on who you're talking to, I'd have to wait close to 15 years after taking that class before my first child was born. But, as every parent knows, it's well worth it. My son Roman came into this world after an emergency C-section delivery, thanks to an extreme lack of oxygen caused by a shortened umbilical cord.

But because of the C-section, I was able to spend the first two hours of his life holding him alone in a quiet waiting room. As I've told him many times, it was there that I programmed his computer for life. I told him all that I felt he would need to know as he was about to navigate his own journey.

As the years have passed, I've realized that I was the one getting my computer reprogrammed. Because at that point in my life, sitting in that quiet waiting room, I was no longer waiting. My life as a father had begun, and I had a new companion for the rest of my journey.

KID PARTY CLOWN

The kid party. Those of you who are parents know the (unnecessary) amount of time, effort, stress, and money that goes into throwing the perfect party for your children these days. Growing up, I only had one birthday where I was allowed to invite friends for a party. It was my seventh birthday, and I invited over five buddies. There was no bounce house, no magician, no DJ, no wanna-be-actor dressed like Twerking Elmo. Nope, just cake, ice cream, and my friends, and it was awesome. The biggest splurge we had was that the ice cream was Neapolitan, so I guess we weren't entirely guilt-free.

Not sure when all of this changed so drastically, but my first introduction to it was when my son Roman was three and got invited to his friend's birthday party in Pacific Palisades. The boy's father and I were also friends, so I had reasonably high hopes that the party would be a good time for me as well.

The backyard was decked out with all the necessary birthday accoutrements, including a Disney-themed bounce house. The open-air detached garage had an amazing sushi display, plus pizza and chicken nuggets for the kids, as well as the prerequisite vegan spread. Because it was L.A. after all, and God forbid your kid was the one labeled as "the boy who had no crudité at his party." In the corner of the garage was where all of the moms were huddled, not because of the crudité, but because of the rosé. Yep, wine and a keg of beer, because nothing screams perfect three-year-old birthday shindig louder than ice cream and Natty Ice.

The party was in full swing when "the entertainment" arrived. He was half an hour late, but none of the kids cared once the much-anticipated Winnie the Pooh stepped foot into the backyard. The kids cheered and I punctuated those cheers with a sashimi spit take worthy of an Academy Award. The reason being, Winnie the Pooh looked more like Vinnie the Pooh who had just rolled in from a hard night of honey dippin'.

Seriously, the fur on his suit was more matted and dirty than a carpeted jetway at LaGuardia. There was also a good four inches of separation from the end of his Pooh arm to his paw. The amount of visible hair in that area alone led me to believe Vinnie was either in witness protection or could possibly be the missing link. Then there were his eyes. The only way to describe them is to say they looked like the result of a one-night stand between Cookie Monster and Steve Buschimi.

All of that being said, the kids genuinely seemed to enjoy his plethora of Poohness during the party, but it's what took place after that struck me as a bit odd. Pooh was officially off the clock and he motioned to my friend to meet him on the side of the garage. There he collected his check for a job . . . done and apparently also requested to stay a bit longer to grab some food. So my friend happily obliged. Vinnie promised that even though he was off the clock, his Pooh head would remain on for the sake of the children. Look at that Johnny Depp–like commitment to character, you go Pooh.

At this point, my son had fallen asleep in my arms, so I was standing alone about 20 feet away from everyone and it was the perfect vantage point for what I was about to witness. From there, I saw Pooh enter the garage and exchange greetings with the giddy wine moms. Not sure what he said, but they were all entranced as they looked at him. It was truly bizarre; they were gazing at him like he was Brad Pitt in *Meet Joe Black*. Actually for all I know, it's L.A., maybe it was Brad, it would've made more sense. He then grabbed a Solo cup and filled it from the keg, strategically tilting back his Pooh head just enough to simultaneously hide his face and fill his gullet with the suds. He then leaned forward and said something that made the wine moms giggle like teenage girls would after hearing Justin Bieber say a word like "poot."

This continued on for a good 10 minutes and after sliding a slice or two of pizza, plus another brew, under his dome, I couldn't help but wonder . . . just what the hell is he saying to these women? I mean, at one point they were pulling out phones and I assume, exchanging numbers for potential party gigs. But maybe not, maybe Tigger was always coming home late from work and they were fed up and wanted Pooh to tap that honey? Who knows? It was genuinely baffling.

I wanted to go and get a beer just to eavesdrop, but chose not to because I couldn't live with myself if I potentially cockblocked Winnie the Pooh. Plus, it may have led to a ban from other kid parties, so I kept my distance. When he finally left, a few of the women huddled up to apparently dish about their honey bear and I just stood there alone, holding my sleeping son and wondering what the hell I had just witnessed.

A year or so later and after telling this story a hundred times, I was inspired to write a television comedy script based on the character that I encountered that day. Needless to say, *Kid Party Clown* was not picked up by any network. The most common notes I received on the script were "too dark," "this wouldn't happen," and "make it more realistic." Maybe the problem was, it was too realistic? Maybe all of the network executives who make these decisions know what occurred on that day of the Pooh and they wanted to keep it quiet, because they have parties to throw as well. Illuminati? No, more like Poohminati... confirmed. Makes me long for the days of slurping up some semi-melted Neapolitan.

THE UNITED COLORS OF CORTESE

As a parent, I've always tried to find the most appropriate and opportunistic times to have those specific "talks" with my kids. I'd rather that when I have a "talk" or "the talk" with them, that they occur organically as opposed to forcing the conversation, like they did on 1960s television shows. "Wally, Beaver, have a seat on the couch so we can talk about that thing that will make you go blind if you do it."

One day I was in my car waiting in the pickup line at Our Lady of Malibu school... that's not a joke, the name of the school really is Our Lady of Malibu. I guarantee it was the only Catholic school on the planet where you could simultaneously see Julia Roberts talking with teachers while Charlie Sheen hit on them. Too bad Aaron Spelling had passed on, because this one had hit written all over it.

Little did I know that day, I'd have one of those opportunities to have a "talk" with my kids about an important life topic. I followed the appropriate pickup and drop-off etiquette, being sure not to hit an orange cone, block a lane, or dare I say, exit my vehicle. I did not need to get ripped a new one again by the P.E. teacher or self-proclaimed "head of school moms" Jan, who was running late for a filler appointment. Note to Jan: Lay off the fillers, girl. Check the damn mirror, pretty sure you're full.

With a successful pickup achieved, my daughter India, first grade, and son Roman, fourth grade, safely in tow, I was ready to hear about the highlights of their day. So what better way to do that than to take them to get some ice cream. It seemed like just your average day—that was, until India decided, through the space in her front teeth and with the slightest lisp, to ask a question I didn't see coming.

"Dad, what color are we?" After a somewhat stereotypical dad laugh from the driver's seat, I asked her to clarify what she meant. India explained herself. "Well, today Camille said that she and I were the only two black girls in class." Now, before I go any further it would help to know, Camille's mother is white and her father is a French black man. India followed this up by saying, "So, are we black?"

As we pulled up to the ice cream shop, I parked the car and in all of my proud parental wisdom thought, "What a perfect opportunity to have an important discussion about race." But I also wanted the kids to come to a conclusion themselves, as opposed to just me answering the question in a very black and white fashion . . . yeah, that was on purpose.

So I said, "Well, your race is determined by the races of your parents. What color is your mom?" India looked out of the back window for a little longer than I had anticipated, put some actual first grade thought into her response, and said, "Orange." I wanted to crack up, but she was dead damn serious. So, I gave her another shot at it. "You think your mother is orange?" "Yessir, her skin is."

This "talk" had taken a bit of a turn, but I still had confidence that a lesson could eventually be found somewhere in the outcome. So I said, "OK, well, what color am I?" and without hesitation, a glance out the window or even a breath, she said, "You're black." I thought to myself, "Damn, maybe that casting director at MTV knew more than I gave her credit for."

I followed up India's response hoping for her to explain her answer, "Do you really think I'm black?" to which she simply replied, "Yep." Then as I smiled to myself, Roman, who was always a kind, reserved boy said, "Well, your skin is darker than President Obama's." Now, in Roman's defense, this was in my single-dad days and I was a big fan of the tan. During that time, if my skin was one shade lighter it would've been called "leather."

"Okay, so you guys are orange and black, like some cool tigers." For the moment both of them were pretty into being tigers, so I thought, why not piggyback on the good vibes with a sprinkle of *Father Knows Best*. "Truth is, guys, it doesn't matter if you've got stripes like a tiger, spots like a leopard, what color your skin is, or what you look like. What matters is if you're a good person and nice to other people. It's what's inside a person that counts."

Both of them sat and thought for a second, probably wishing they were still tigers. So I tried another angle to clarify it with something that was a little less cliché, hoping they would understand a bit better. So I said, "It's like ice cream. It doesn't matter what color or flavor it is, all of it is good, right?" They happily nodded in agreement, and as India opened her door to exit the car she said, "Yep, and we're chocolate!" Ward Clever 2.0? Maybe not, but it was a valiant effort.

WAiTiNG FOR My REAL LiFE TO BEGiN

A few years ago, I was invited by a good friend to go see Thomas "She Blinded Me with Science" Dolby in concert at The Canyon Club in Agoura Hills, California. To set the table for you, the interior of the club looks as if it hasn't been updated since 1972, but yet it has this odd magnetism of yesteryear attached to it that makes it extremely hard to stay away. The main ingredient of that magnetism is still supplied by the fact that a good majority of the bands that play there, while still beloved, aren't quite as popular as they once were.

It truly is one of the last places around where you can sit at your weathered red pleather booth eating dinner while you watch a concert. That's right, nothing quite like enjoying a semi-flavorful steak while simultaneously enjoying the musical flavors of Meatloaf. It may sound odd to some, but that's the kind of place we're talking about here, and it was pretty awesome.

My friend thought Thomas Dolby was slated to go on at 9 p.m., so we rolled in at the tragically hip-middle-aged-white-guy-almost-bedtime time of 8:58 p.m. Yeah, we had it like that. As we walked through the doors all we heard was Thomas singing at the top of his lungs "SCIENCE," then the big finish, and the crowd went crazy! Wait, "Science"?! Why would Thomas Dolby start the show with his biggest hit? He wouldn't. The show started at 8, not 9. Thomas had already blinded everyone, and he was out.

At that point, there wasn't much we could do other than laugh at our misfortune. Once the lights went up, we did some serious people watching at a crowd that could have easily been cast as extras in the *Star Wars* cantina bar scene. Luckily, there was another act following Thomas, so we grabbed a few drinks and waited for Colin Hay to take the stage. For those of you who don't know, Colin was the frontman for the group Men at Work in the 80s and more than likely was the man who introduced 99 percent of you to a "vegemite sandwich."

Once Colin took the stage, his talent was apparent and his solo acoustic material was addicting. If you don't believe me, just ask Sir Paul McCartney, who was in a tiny roped-off area next to the bathrooms dancing on top of a table. Yep, the two celebrities at a dinner club watching Colin Hay perform were The Mimbo and a Beatle—sounds like a 70s cop drama on CBS from the creator of *Jake and The Fatman*. I seriously can't tell you how many times I've thought just how odd that entire evening was. I felt like I was in some sort of parallel universe, but it was running five seconds behind actual time.

Toward the end of his set, Colin performed his song "Waiting for My Real Life to Begin." I'd never heard the song prior to that night, but it was a beautiful, engaging song, which I instantly related to. Once I was home after the show, I downloaded it immediately. Over the course of the next year of my life, it kind of became my personal anthem. I'd listen to it at least once a day.

To me, the message of the song basically speaks of someone who knows better things are right around the corner. He's dreamt of them happening and he's anxiously waiting for that moment to arrive, but it never does. Some may see it as a song of despair, I saw it as a song of hope. Probably because I was at a place not just in my professional life, but more so in my personal life, where I was "hoping" for things to get better. Unfortunately, in my heart I honestly knew they wouldn't.

For many years I was in a relationship that filled my life with toxicity. Continually hiding it from the world was a burdensome weight I could no longer carry. I had reached a point where I refused to continue down the path that I was on. My children will always be my everything, but deep down inside, I knew I was at a crossroad on my journey, and a life-altering decision was necessary for myself, as well as for them.

It was unfair for my kids to grow up watching a poor imitation of what a "happy" life was. So, I knew it was time for a change because I'd never forgive myself if they were to then repeat that broken cycle in their own relationships. I believe you're supposed to show you children the proper way to live life, no matter how much pain you may have to endure to do so. It's called being a parent.

In trying to manage my life from that point on, I would often think of the Canyon Club night and realize the reason I was there on that odd evening. I came to the conclusion that it was the universe's way of letting me know, there's nothing wrong with wanting your real life to begin. I just needed to stop *waiting* for it to begin. Get busy living or get busy dying.

The next few years of my life was an extremely difficult progression that culminated in a life-changing, literal "man in the mirror" moment. In the end, I came out the other side being a single father, which at the time was definitely what I wanted. My children and I endured a lot of pain over that span, but we garnered strength from having gone through it, learned from it, and realized that when it comes to love, you should never compromise. As painful as that process was, I'd finally reached a point where I could now be truly open and honest with myself and my children. I was finally free to be the father I always knew I could be, which was the best thing for all of us.

Anyone who has experienced extreme personal pain knows that it's worthy of an entire book in itself. Thankfully, this is not that book. It's silly for me to think I could tell any of you something you don't already know. The truth is, each and every one of us comes equipped with all the necessary knowledge we need to navigate this lifetime. The issue lies in being brave enough to use that knowledge to confront our pain and, in doing so, allowing ourselves to learn from that confrontation. Having the strength to come to that realization allowed me to move forward with my life in the most positive way possible and to write this book.

There's one thought regarding all of this that I've shared with my children, and I'd like to share it with you.

There is a purpose to the pain.

Embrace that thought. Hell, go ahead and make out with it if you want. Just don't ever forget it. Trust me, the more you peel back that pain and embrace its purpose and why it exists, you'll not only heal but you'll find strength and happiness buried deep inside that had been waiting for you. That smile on your heart is there for a reason, be sure to appreciate the fact that you've earned it and allow yourself to happily move forward with gratitude, thanks and positivity. Now, back to our regularly scheduled programming.

HOW TO? NOPE. HOW I DO!

As I stated near the beginning of this book, one of the initial angles discussed was to write it as a "How To" book. That just didn't feel right to me, I would've been more comfortable writing a "How Not To" book. (Actually, put a pin in that idea for later.) On a conference call with the publishers, I expressed to them that I don't know "how to," but I do know "how I do," and that works for me. Honestly, I'm not the type of person who feels the need to tell anyone how to do anything. But, if you want to brainstorm and figure something out, I'm your guy.

The following are a few beliefs that I do my best to adhere to as a parent, partner, and person. I also, on a daily basis, try to implore my children to follow them as well. But, I've found the best way to do that is by showing them, not telling them. This is "How I Do":

1. HONESTY: Pretty obvious one, but any of us who have been to emotional hell and back, eventually come to the conclusion that the only and best way to live your life is to be completely honest. To live your life any other way is a waste of precious energy. First and foremost, you must be 100 percent with yourself. None of this 99 percent b.s., because, as we all know, that rapidly falls to 50 percent, then you're off the rails. As a parent, if you're not being honest with yourself, then you're not being honest with your kids and/or your significant other. Plus, when you're honest, you never have to remember anything. "Babe, it's your birthday? Oh damn, I forgot... no seriously, I'm being honest." Okay, bad example, but you know what I mean. Make your life easier and start by being true to you first.

2. CHECK YOURSELF: Hot on the heels of honesty, I've found this one to be a must and is, without a doubt, the first thing I do prior to addressing any situation. No matter what type of conflict I may be dealing with, the first person I always check, before any type of rebuttal, is myself. "How did this come about?" "Am I the one causing the conflict?" "Did I do something, whether intentionally or unintentionally, to get it to this point?" Once you can HONESTLY check yourself in any type of situation, then you can move forward toward a resolution.

3. POSITIVITY: Sounds simple, but as many of you can relate to on certain days, it's not always easy to be Positive Guy. I work very hard to be a "glass-half-full" person, but some

days I'm more of a "I'm just happy I've got a glass" kind of guy. I'll be the first to tell you that, by the day's end, Carolina and the kids are tired of me eavesdropping on conversations only to randomly yell "positivity!" from the other side of the house, just in case I feel they're getting a bit off track. Annoying? Yes, positively annoying. But it's 100 percent better than the alternative. Actually, if we did a reality show from our house, people who watched would make a drinking game out of it. "Dude, Dan just said 'positivity' again, so you need to chug another Zima!"

4. ADMIT WHEN YOU'RE WRONG: This is one of the most important things I've learned to do as a parent. When I screw up, I take accountability, from the smallest things to the largest. If it's on me, I step up. "My bad, guys." "I was wrong." "That's my fault." "I'll do my best to make sure that doesn't happen again." "I shouldn't have worn the red leather pants to Christmas mass." However you want to say it, just say it. It's important for me as a father to be strong enough to admit when I'm wrong, but even more important for the kids to hear it from me. When there's accountability for the head of a household, then everyone else understands that it's an even playing field. It should never be about "me," it should always be about "us" as a family.

5. LIVE IN THE MOMENT: I know I wrote about this before, but to me it's extremely important to encourage my children to do this as well. To appreciate all that life is teaching us as it occurs, the good as well as the bad. If they absorb as much as they can now, they'll begin to appreciate how beautiful life actually is at a much earlier age. Although, it's not always the easiest concept to sell my daughter the day of an AP Euro History exam.

6. LEARN FROM YOUR MISTAKES: Sounds simple, but so many of us don't do this, and we repeatedly find ourselves in the same unfortunate situations. The amount of what I've learned about life from my successes is not even close to what I've learned from my mistakes. So, this has been very important for me to get my children to embrace. There's a reason everything happens. Why not be open and aware as to why it does? Learn from what the mistake was, the consequences of it, and do your best to not repeat it. Bad example: While shooting an episode of *MTV Sports* with Dean Cain and NFL Hall of Fame Linebacker and extremely huge man Junior Seau, I dared Junior to slap me in the face when the cameras started rolling. He happily obliged, split my lip on camera, and the only thing I could hear through the intense ringing in my ear was Dean giggling like a six-year-old girl who just heard Elmo fart. Since that day, I've made it a point not to dare any linebackers to slap me in the face. Lesson learned; further similar mistakes avoided.

7. EARMUFFS: If there's one thing I've learned from my life in general thanks to working in Hollywood, it's to not listen to negative things people say about you. Again, something that is much easier said than done, especially when you've got critics writing things like "The fact that Dan Cortese still works is proof that the devil keeps his promises." (Gotta admit, I thought that one was pretty creative.) But it becomes even more difficult when you're trying to get your children to follow this mantra as well. Then add social media bullies into the mix and the negativity that fills the air seems to outweigh the positivity on a daily basis. Sadly, this has become our reality in the world today. You cannot allow someone else's words or actions to control your emotions. Ultimate strength is found in silence, and in that silence

you not only control yourself but also the negativity thrust upon you. So shhhhhh . . .

8. ME FIRST: One thing that I'm adamant about as a father is having an "open door" policy when it comes to the kids having to deal with certain life situations they may happen to find themselves in. I always tell them, no matter how bad it seems, ALWAYS come to me first, be honest with me about what happened and let's figure everything out together. No matter what they did, I'd be more upset if they didn't come to me for guidance than I would for whatever it was that occurred.

9. WHO'S HOUSE? FUN HOUSE: We don't go to parties; the party comes to us. This is one of the most important things to me in life. I didn't have a lot growing up, but the one thing we did have in our house was F-U-N. This is a mandatory requirement at Casa Cortese. It's not just about our rap battles, roast battles, dance parties, or even the disco lights in the kitchen. We could be cooking dinner, doing homework, or just chillin' on the couch . . . no matter what the circumstance, we always have FUN in our house. I've found that this is easily achieved when you follow numbers 1 through 8. Always remember, laughter is the fuel for a long life.

TAKING MATTERS INTO YOUR OWN HANDS

Having children is the most extreme adventure any of us could ever experience, and I should know—I hosted *MTV Sports* (insert rimshot, canned laughter and a Mentos-like freeze-frame here). The joy that being a parent brings into your life is unparalleled by any other experience, but some of the changes that accompany that joy can throw the best of us off of our game.

Any couple who's had a child can attest to the fact that there's one aspect of their relationship that really, shall we say, dries up a bit after kids enter the picture. If they don't agree with mc, they're either lying or they're lying. That's right, I'm talking about loading the clown into the canon, the freaky deaky, or, as Salt and Pepa said, "Let's talk about sex, baby."

Sex doesn't completely cease when you have a child; it comes to more of a rolling stop. A rolling stop that's barely moving, but stopped enough that you'd still pass your driver's test. Because of these types of issues and others associated with being a parent, many couples are forced to get creative when it comes to finding time to . . . "relax."

A few summers back, I took my children to a beach near where I live in Malibu called Little Dume. It's a private beach that's very well known for the many A-List celebrities who adorn it. For the record, I don't consider myself an A-Lister like those folks, I'm more of an Ayyyyy lister, and I don't "adorn" it, I bring more of a beached whale with a beer and boombox vibe to the sand.

That particular day, I was standing alone at the water's edge watching my kids duck waves with friends when I was approached by a certain rock star who I immediately recognized. Now, for the sake of the story and its content, I can't divulge who it was. That being said, for the rest of the chapter I'll just refer to him as "Jick Magger." Okay, for the record, it wasn't Mick, but that name kind of made me laugh.

Jick was there watching his kids as well and as we started talking, I was flattered to find out the reason he approached me was because he was a fan of *MTV Sports*. He also expressed that he felt like he "knew me" since he grew up watching me. Again, I was flattered, so I in turn spewed some butt-kissing rhetoric of my own to let him know that I was also a fan of his.

With all of the bro-love out of the way, we began talking about typical dad stuff. How many kids we had, boys or girls, ages, you know, average dad small talk. Then out of nowhere the dirty diaper hit the fan. He asked for my opinion on something that had happened between him and his wife earlier that morning.

Jick sprung into a story about how when he woke up that morning, he was feeling rather lascivious. Then he started talking so fast, the only thing I really understood was when he slowed his speech to enunciate the words *morning wood*; then he was off to the races again. He ended his ramble by telling me that his wife basically shut down his advances because their kids were awake. Now, just like all of us guys do when we get shut down, he sulked like a dog who thought he was going on a walk but was really going to the vet.

With this, the rock star told me he laid alone in his bed on a Saturday morning and accepted the reality of his situation. He then told me once his wife went to tend to their children he "was left with no other choice" but to take matters into his own hands or . . . hand. After resolving said matter, Jick fell asleep (no surprise there), only to be awakened by his wife 15 minutes later. She informed him the kids were watching *Sesame Street* and they had a 10-minute "boom-boom window," and punctuated it with a "So hurry up and do this." Amazing how the sexy talk devolves once the kids are in the picture, right?

Jick then boldly did what any good husband would do; he told his wife the truth. He then proceeded to let her know that he was going to need his own 15-minute "recovery window" before he would be physically capable of climbing through her boom-boom window. In his words, "She went ape shit." I never really understood that phrase, but I assume it's on par with "bat shit," which is also just some other shit I never understood.

Then in a very *Young and the Restless* manner, she let him know how wrong he was, and before he could respond, she stormed out of the room, slamming the door to punctuate her point. (A little side note ladies: In situations like that, guys like to act like they get upset that they didn't have a chance to speak up for themselves. But the truth of the matter is, they're just happy you left the room. Sorry fellas, it's time they knew.)

Jick then told me their argument continued on, and in telling it, was waving his arms so violently, I thought he chose to accompany the story with some kind of funky interpretive dance.

Jick: "What did I do that was so wrong?"
Mrs. Jick: "What you did was just like cheating on me!"
Jick: "Actually, it's way better than cheating, because I was alone. Plus, now when we go to the beach, I won't be looking at other girls, so you should be thanking me."
Mrs. Jick: "So that's what you do when you go to the beach? You look at other girls?"

Boom, just like that, the focus of the argument had changed, and there was no way he could win. As I stood there listening to this, all I kept thinking was, "I just met this guy and he's spilling his guts to me. Maybe I should be a therapist?!" Jick continued his story, timing it perfectly to end it right as my 10-year-old daughter ran out of the waves and put her arm around me. I was thankful, because that story would've been a tough one for daddy to explain.

Jick buttoned his vent with, "So, be totally honest with me Dan, do you think I did anything wrong?" To me, this was like the chicken and the egg conundrum, so I did what every guy in my position would have wisely done. I agreed with him, because I didn't want any "hands-on" details brought up in front of my daughter, and most importantly, I was holding out hope for some backstage V.I.P. passes at Lollapalooza.

Look, if you're in a relationship and have children, many of you have probably experienced similar situations. A lot of us have seen the three times a day morph into three times a month, morph into three minutes in the closet. Truth is, as a parent one of the most important things you learn is how to adapt. Because your life will never be the same again, and a good majority of it will be lived on the fly.

You're like the aging NBA big man who can no longer dunk, so you learn to shoot three pointers and extend your career by five years. You don't play as often as you once did, so when you get a chance to enter the game for a few minutes, you let those shots fly. If any of you have a better solution, please let me know. In the meantime, Carolina and I will continue adapting with the "Baby can you come out to the garage and help me for a second?" method.

TO INTERNET OR INTERNOT, THAT'S THE QUESTION?

As a parent, we're always looking for ways to impart wisdom on our children, and as our parents did before us, we tend to use examples from our childhood. That being said, whatever happened to the good old days of having to work for something? You would work hard, reap the rewards, and appreciate that you'd accomplished something. It's a difficult value to instill in kids these days, because access to everything is literally at their fingertips. I recently expressed my concern to my friend Tony from Queens, who uses words like "gabagool," and he said, "I'll tell you what happened . . . Google happened. When I was a kid, if you had told me to "Google" someone, I would've been like, no freakin' way, I don't roll like that."

A perfect example of this took place a little while back as I was attempting to help my son with a report for middle school. I told him how when I had reports to do, my mother used to take me to the library and I'd be there for hours using things like encyclopedias, the Dewey Decimal System, and microfiche to do all of the research. He looked at me almost the same way people did that time I was spotted at a Barry Manilow concert in Vegas. His response was simple: "Why didn't you just Google it, Dad?" There it was, the separation of generations. Badda-bing-badda-boom, Tony from Queens was right.

A few weeks later, I was at a Halloween party discussing the same dilemma with a rather heavyset guy dressed as a pregnant nun who insisted on being called "Sister Richard." He looked as if Dee Snyder from Twisted Sister and 80s Roseanne Barr spawned a drunk manchild. If nothing else, I respected his commitment to his costume and his tequila.

With bean dip remains in his teeth, Sister Richard slurred out his thoughts as eloquently as a grown drunk man dressed as a pregnant nun with bean dip in his teeth possibly could. "When you were a young boy and you wanted to see a naked girl, what did you have to do?" I immediately started scanning the room for someone else to have a conversation with. "You'd have to make a conscious decision that this was your main objective for the day. Then you'd get on your stolen Schwinn, ride across town to your single uncle's apartment, hide your bike in the bushes right next to his old rusted-out van, and peer through the kitchen window to see if he was home. Once you realized the coast was clear, you'd jimmy the window open, climb in, and hit the floor like a Navy Seal ready to make Bin Laden squeal." I have to admit, at this point, I was hooked and had to hear him out.

"Like the wind, you would stealthily make your way to his bathroom, taking care not to knock over his Old Spice teetering on the sink. Then just behind the weathered-looking toilet bowl you spot his magazine rack. Your fingers rifled through all his *Sports Illustrated*'s so quickly that they would have made Liberace pop a rhinestone on his pants."

"And then, you hit the jackpot. Quickly you give one last glance over your shoulder to assure your safety, before you pull out … a *Playboy*. But not just "a" *Playboy*. "The" *Playboy*. She's tattered and torn, but like a fine wine, somehow seems better with age. You open it, and like Casanova on a Courtesan, have a little private time with Stacks, from *BJ and the Bear*."

"Suddenly you hear the key in the front door and you become a ninja. You dust for prints, snag a quick hit off the Old Spice, and with a knowing smile on your face, the carefully planned steps you took to start the mission play out in rapid reverse. Then, almost as if it were a dream, you find yourself back in the comfort of your own bed, knowing that today you worked hard, reaped the rewards, and accomplished what you set out to do."

I thought about it for a second, first wondering, "How is this guy not in prison?" My next thought was, "I need a new circle of friends." But then I realized, in some perversely odd fashion, his story made quite a bit of sense. I said, "You know, you're right, that's how it should be. We need to instill that work ethic in our kids. Not that particular type of work, but the ethic of work itself." Sister Richard downed the rest of the tequila, smiled as he leaned in close to me, and said in a hushed tone, "Bullshit. Why work for it when you don't have to? It's the American way." I guess that generational separation isn't as wide as I thought.

SOCIAL (DISTORTION) MEDIA

Those of you who have children know that our journey as parents never ends. We will forever be "mom" or "dad," and no matter your child's age, they will always be your baby. So, as I sit here writing this, I realize we're at a crossroads, the likes of which have never been seen before in history. We can't rely on our parents to help us out with this problem because they didn't have to deal with it. All thanks to the rapid emergence and "importance" of social media.

It's difficult to "parent" around these waters because we're wading into the pool at the same time as our children. Unfortunately we can't hold their hands along the way because we're trying to stay afloat as well. They're growing up with problems we never had to deal with. As silly as it sounds, a few of the biggest one's are "followers" and "likes." Truth is, they are neither. Just as there's nothing truly social about social media. This is proven by the fact that interacting with our phones has replaced good old-fashioned human interaction.

As we try to support our own children in this new era, we must also become self-aware with how we conduct ourselves "socially." More simply put, if you don't want your daughter posting booty pics, then you should refrain from posting them as well, mom. No matter how good your yoga gal pal Turnt Tammy says you look.

Being in the profession I'm in, I'm not only encouraged to have social media pages, many times I'm contractually obligated to use them to promote projects. Like this book, for example. I'll be all over social media promoting my bandanna-wearing butt off. So, feel free to take a break from reading and follow me on Insta and Twitter @dancortese. The first 20 new followers will get a photo of a signed copy of my book DM'd to them and as an added bonus, I'll insert their favorite emoji into the message. Sad but true; this is the type of world we live in today.

So, I find myself walking a fine line with my kids. How can I tell them that it's not important how many "likes" and "followers" you have, when I'm expected to increase mine? As job opportunities present themselves to me, so often getting the gig or not hinges on my "social numbers." I can't tell you how many times I've wanted to say, "Here's a social number for you," and button that with an Italian salute. So, I deal with it the only way I can. I lean on my honesty with the kids and reassure them as often as needed that no number of "likes" should ever affect the love they have for themselves.

That's all fine and they appreciate it. But when they see random 16-year-olds doing make-up tutorials or pranking people in malls, getting 50 million hits and "likes," and driving Teslas, kids can't help but think they'd like to have all of that, too. Therefore, my argument to them needed to become a bit stronger. But I've realized that was the problem, I don't need to make an argument at all, so I've chosen to rely on our trust. Trust that they will respectfully use the platforms and in doing so, prioritize their self-worth over their "status". My job is to let them know that we're in this together and I'm here to help guide them along this path, not insist on what direction they must go.

One aspect of social media where I've found I can be extremely helpful is in dealing with internet bullies and trolls. Sorry, but every time I hear someone use the term internet "troll," I can't help but think of a troll doll and assume, "They can't be that bad." But alas, they are, and I've encountered my fair share of them thanks to what I've chosen to do for a living. I never thought I'd say this but, having to deal with them has been a blessing for me. Because of it, I now have the necessary knowledge to help my kids when it comes to dealing with the different types of negativity that eventually finds everyone on social media.

Trust me, I'll get another healthy dose from the Troll Patrol once this book is released. "Is it a pop-up book? Did Kurt Loder write it for him? Bet it's a whopper of a read! Is it in crayon? Who knew he was still alive? Who cares?" They'll try their best to get one of their "followers" to laugh and hopefully, get a re-tweet. That's fine, it's the world we live in today and I get it, because it's the easy way out. It's how people choose to share their "voice" nowadays. Not in person, not face to face, but from their phone armed with a fake profile pic and a sick handle like @someloser68, because someone equally as cool already had @someloser69.

Truth is, there's nothing anyone can say about me that will ever affect me negatively. I continue to try and get my kids to accept that same mindset. But, I also understand that it's easier for me to do so because, thanks to Hollywood, my skin is thicker than John Stamos's hair after a blowout. I'm not sure if it's intriguing, comical, or just plain sad that people actually take time out of their day to spew random negativity toward others. All I can say to them is, if you have a job, get back to work or try having an actual conversation with a coworker. If you don't have a job, put on your drawers, get out of your grandmama's basement and go outside and get one, because you're giving trolls a bad name.

While in the midst of trying to decipher this new way of "socializing" and "liking" others, I decided to stop wasting my time doing so. I see it like this. As a father I will teach my children right from wrong, to always be respectful, conduct themselves with class, help those who can't help themselves, and always find time to laugh. Because at the end of the day, people are either going to love and appreciate you or not. Simply put, the number of followers you have or likes you get doesn't really matter if you don't love and appreciate yourself.

CHiLL RiDE?
NAH, I'll TAKE THE THRILL RiDE

I've found that after you turn 50, the majority of parents I know understandably look forward to sailing off into the proverbial sunset. Retirement is right around the corner, the kids are grown and almost gone, and you finally get to do what YOU want to do again. They see the light at the end of the tunnel. That's the goal for the majority of people my age, but there's a little snag. First off, why are you in a tunnel? Is it because that's the quickest way to get to your destination? If so, then therein lies the difference between us. I've always embraced the belief that it's more about the journey than the destination. For that reason, I've chosen to skip the tunnel, drive up the front side of the mountain of life, BASE jump off the back, and enjoy the view on the way down.

I guess I'm not like many guys my age—actually, I don't think I'm like any guys my age, or any other age for that matter. To be real, I'm a little weird, it's kind of what I like about me. I think you'll be hard-pressed to find another 52-year-old wearing a Dreft-washed, sleeveless *Wu-Tang Clan* t-shirt and flip flops who's strapped with a toddler in a Baby Bjørn talking Enrico Morricone movie scores in the produce section of Ralph's. Sorry, Whole Foods, I inhaled poison working at a steel mill in Pittsburgh. If that hasn't got me by now, I don't think a nonorganic apple will.

I bring all this up because I find that I'm at a point in my life where I want to put the gas pedal to the floor, not ease up on it. This is the age you want to find out what you've got under the hood, not when you're 21, it's obvious then. It was this mindset that propelled me to ask my life partner-in-all-crimes-good, Carolina, to marry me.

The Cliff Notes version of our relationship goes as follows. We first met through a mutual friend online, but not a dating app, on Instagram...so yeah, a dating app. (This is usually the point where the gossiping begins.) She lived in New York and I was there on a business trip, so I asked her out for drinks. She said yes and gave me the address of a bar to meet her at in the West Village. I got there early, she was late, I realized there were no women in the establishment and thought she may have sent me to a gay bar as a joke, or maybe she was Pauly Shore "catfishing" me. Actually, that would have been pretty damn hilarious.

Luckily, Carolina showed up, perfectly backlit as she entered, almost like that scene of Kelly LeBrock in *Weird Science*, but in a much hotter Colombian way. We immediately hit it

FIGURE 33.1   We got this!

off, went to dinner after drinks, went to drinks after dinner, and I asked her to marry me on a rooftop bar overlooking the sparkling New York City skyline. She said yes and we've been together ever since that day (Figure 33.1). I know, even Evel Knievel was like, "Damn, when homie says he's putting the pedal to the metal, he's not lying!"

The reality of it all is, this is the first adult relationship I've ever been in where my partner puts the kid's needs, as well as mine, ahead of her own. It's something I've always tried to do in my prior relationships, and to experience it finally being reciprocated in such an unselfish, loving way proved to me that she was the One. Or as my grandfather, may he rest in peace, would have said, "She's the cat's ass, Danny!"

As the story is told, in 2019, five years into our fabulous family fun, Roman, India, Carolina, and I welcomed Enzo into our lives to round out the Cortese Crew starting five. Who would have thought that at 51 I would have slipped one past the goalie? Truth is, I didn't care what people thought. I was a father again, and it was just what my heart needed.

After Enzo was born, I noticed something when people would talk to me about becoming a parent again at my age. There were two very cut-and-dried opinions expressed: "Wow, you have two teenagers, you were so close to being done. Are you okay with having another one?" (I always laugh at "Okay with having another one?" like kids are donuts or a shot of tequila or something.) The other opinion, which was from a good majority of the men I talked to, said, "That's pretty damn amazing. I wish I could do it all over again, too!"

It got me to thinking about the first train of thought, and my opinion is simply this. When someone says, "You were almost done" to me, I feel like that's a phrase you use when you're referring to a person's prison sentence ending, not their children moving out. Maybe they just missed the meaning of parenthood the first time around, or maybe they're just the people who are letting up on the gas pedal. Or maybe it's as simple as, they're not me. Which, truthfully, makes the most sense— to each his own. It's how life should be.

In my eyes, parenthood is like the biggest E-ticket roller-coaster you've ever ridden, with the highest of highs and sudden drops that take your breath away. It scares the shit out of you, it makes you hold your breath, makes you laugh, makes you scream, makes you cry, makes you question, "Why did I do this?!" Then, the moment it's over, you catch your breath and smile to yourself when you realize how quickly the ride went by and that you survived it. And as you recollect the amount of incredible emotions you experienced along the way, you wish you could ride it just one more time.

Well, fortunately for me, I just found another five tickets in the front pocket of my 501 jeans and I'm back on board. I rode this wild ride with Roman, I rode it with India, so why not let Enzo take me for an adventure as well? Luckily, I didn't have to wait in line because they let people my age cut it.

As far back as I can remember I wanted to be a father, and now I've been blessed to experience that dream three times over. Nope, there's never a dull moment, especially with one in college, one in high school, and one in diapers. I've become accustomed to simultaneously talking potential career opportunities with Roman, while I "help" India with AP English homework, attempt to stop Enzo from diving off the couch, and give Carolina a kiss on the cheek . . . all while I write this sentence.

Truth is, when my journey comes to an end and I take a peek under the hood of my life, I'll see that while the ride with this crew wasn't always easy, the fun we had sure as hell made it worth it! My tank will be empty, but my soul will be full, knowing that I did my best to give my family all the love that I possibly could.

THE 50-POINT JUMPSHOT

I wanted the last chapter of this book to be called "The 50-Point Jump Shot" for a very specific reason. Many fans of MTV will recognize it as a *Rock n' Jock* basketball reference. Being a staple in those games for the better part of the 90s, I felt it was rather apropos. For those of you who aren't familiar with it, as it sounds, it's a difficult basketball shot at a hoop raised 30 feet in the air. If you make it, it's worth 50 points, and in an instant, you can win a game that seemed all but lost.

Having experienced many of the extreme highs and lows that life has to offer, I've chosen to look at the 50-point jump shot from more of a "Dan" perspective. Metaphorically speaking, I see it as a beacon of hope for anyone who's ever considered giving up. By that I mean, no matter how far behind you may feel you are in life or when all hope seems lost, the fact is, you're never truly out of the game. Unfortunately, more often than not we become so consumed with how bad we think our lives are that we don't realize it only takes one shot to drop and we're right back in it.

It doesn't matter how desperate or impossible the shot may seem. You can't make it if you don't take it. I took one when I was 22 and moved to Los Angeles to chase a dream, and I was fortunate enough to see it drop. I've also taken countless shots since then, I've made some and I've missed some, but more importantly, I never stopped shooting. Now I'm 52 and I'm taking another one by writing this book. I'm not quite sure where it will land, but I know I'm proud of myself for letting it fly. Never stop striving, never stop trying, never stop believing, and never, ever give up on yourself.

When I started the process of putting this document together, the goal was for me to openly and honestly look back at my life and see if I truly am the person I thought I was. In doing so, I rediscovered a few things about myself. I didn't forget these aspects of my life, but probably ignored them more often than I should have. So after that realization, I've made it a point to keep them in the forefront of my day-to-day living, because I feel they are the cornerstones that help to define me as a man.

Dan ... The Man

1. Don't stress about what may happen next, when you can appreciate right now.
2. Always be thankful for what you **DO** have, instead of obsessing over all that you don't.

3. Pray for strength and guidance. In doing so, always remember to be aware enough to realize when they are given to you.

4. Don't let others mistake my humor for ignorance or my kindness for weakness.

5. Why me? Only ask this during the good times as opposed to the bad. The recognition and appreciation of good fortune will regenerate more of it into your life.

6. Always try new things. Don't ever say, "Do you know how old I'll be by the time I'll learn to do that?" Yes I do—the same age you'll be anyway, so just do it!

7. Stop being one of the boys and be a man. (This goes for the ladies as well.) It doesn't mean stop having fun, get a new set of friends, or change your life entirely. It means being strong enough to recognize the importance of prioritizing your life appropriately.

8. Instead of "picking your battles," try not having any at all. A battle is, more often than not, a confrontation that could have been avoided. And a war usually stems from an unnecessary battle.

9. Only take life seriously when it is serious. Even then, when the winds have died down, find any and every opportunity to allow yourself to find some humor in it and laugh. Remember, there is a purpose to the pain.

10. The most important decision you'll ever have to make in this life is how you choose to live it! Once you make that decision, all the others are relatively easy. (Via my father, via his mother.)

10a. I was voted Best Male Dancer in ninth grade. I guess watching *Soul Train* all those Saturdays paid off. (Sorry, but had to squeeze that nugget into this book somewhere.)

As I sit here, with the entire puzzle of my life pieced back together, the question is, does it look like what I thought it would? At the beginning of the book, I stated that one of the reasons I decided to write it was because "how I perceive myself, how I think others perceive me, and how others actually do perceive me, are more than likely, three entirely separate views." What I've discovered was this: who you are isn't defined by another person's opinion of you, no matter how hard people or platforms like social media try to make us believe this today. Everyone perceives individuals in their own unique fashion, but it doesn't play any part in determining the real you.

Because a name, a rumor, a photo, an opinion, a "like," or even a character I've played doesn't define who I am. I am defined by my actions—how I treat my family, friends, colleagues, strangers on the street, and people in need. Others will undoubtedly draw their own conclusions from that, but it's their conclusion, not mine. They'll choose to use words in any positive or negative way they see fit, and as long as I see fit not to let their words affect me, then I am in control of who I am. Not who I was yesterday or who I'm going to be tomorrow, but who I AM RIGHT NOW. Because when you embrace what's happening in the moment, you control the moment, and when you control the moment, you are then in control of your life. Only you can determine who you are.

So, what's the verdict: Who am I? Am I "MTV's Dan Cortese," the Mimbo, the in-your-face Whopper Guy, a *Melrose Place* thug, or just some guy who loves to have fun and laugh until he cries with his wife and kids? Truth is, I'm just a man who's constantly trying to love, learn, and evolve in every aspect of his life. A man who has a simple, yet somewhat difficult goal for himself at the end of every day. It is that when tomorrow comes, I will make sure that I am a better version of the man that I was the day prior.

Having gone through this entire process I've discovered something else. As important as it was for me to understand who I was, I felt it was just as important for me to let you know who I am. Remember, if you don't like the narrative of your story, become the narrator.

Finally, if there is one last thought I'd like to leave with whomever is reading this right now, it would be this. Make sure to embrace **ALL** of your life along the way, not just the good but the bad as well. Because each and every moment we experience is equally as important as the one before it. One of the most beautiful things I've learned about life is that once you find the strength to allow yourself to embrace **ALL** of who you truly are, you can finally let go of all that has held you down. So, let go and let's go! I can't think of a better way to do that than to . . . *Step off!*

ACKNOWLEDGMENTS

I want to genuinely thank my editing team at Wiley for their guidance and inspiration throughout this entire creative process. I would also like to give special thanks to Wiley Senior Vice President and Executive Publisher Matt Holt for seeing something in me that I didn't see in myself. Having never written a book before, my trepidation was obvious, but Matt had unwavering faith in me and trusted that I would deliver a product we could all be proud of.

To all three of my children, Roman, India, and Enzo. Thank you for supporting me and for genuinely being interested in my progression as I worked my way through the challenge of writing this. If you weren't interested, you faked it really, really well. Truthfully, you were an integral part of this book. Think about it, it would've been so weird to write a book about parenting if I didn't have children. In all honesty, you were my inspiration for doing this the right way, and hopefully in doing so, I made you proud. I love the three of you more than you'll ever know.

Finally, the one person who put up with the most throughout the duration of the writing of this book was my soulmate, Carolina. Any time she would walk within a 20-foot radius of me while I was writing, she knew she was about to get bombarded with questions like, "Babe, can I read this to you?" "Boo, does this make sense?" Every time I would doubt myself, you patiently and lovingly got me back on track with your belief in me. Thank you, not only for your unwavering support and always loving me unconditionally but also for loving me enough to give me honest notes and ideas throughout this process. I know for a fact that I could not have completed this book without you by my side. I love you eternally with all that I am. You are my one, only, and forever muse.

ABOUT THE AUTHOR

Dan Cortese shot to stardom as the extreme host of the two-time Emmy-Award-winning *MTV Sports*. For six successful years, Dan interviewed and interacted with the largest stars from the worlds of sports and entertainment. He then went on to star in NBC's remake of the cult classic *Route 66*. Next on his plate, Dan starred in the CBS drama *Traps* with Academy-Award winner George C. Scott. After that, he kept the ball rolling and co-starred on the hit NBC sitcom *Veronica's Closet*, opposite Emmy winner Kirstie Alley. From there, he continued creating laughs, starring in the sitcoms *Rock Me Baby* and *What I Like About You*.

Cortese's numerous television credits also include memorable guest-starring roles. Dan appeared in one of the highest-rated episodes of *Seinfeld* ever as Tony, Elaine's "Mimbo" boyfriend that George had a "man crush" on. The darker side of Dan's acting chops were on display for a season when he portrayed the evil Jess Hanson on *Melrose Place*. He also had memorable turns on *Andy Richter Controls the Universe*, *The Single Guy*, and *Hot In Cleveland* with the legendary Betty White.

Cortese has appeared in many feature films, including *Demolition Man*, opposite Sylvester Stallone and Sandra Bullock,

Weekend in the Country with Jack Lemmon and Dudley Moore, and *After Sex* with Brooke Shields. In addition he starred in the made-for-television movies *The Triangle* for TBS and NBC's spin on the Shirley Jackson classic, *The Lottery*.

When not acting, Dan continued to keep his hosting skills sharp by helming, NBC's *My Dad Is Better Than Your Dad*, ABC's action-packed *Crash Course*, and the fun-filled *Guinness World Records: Unleashed* for TruTV.

A native of Pittsburgh, Pennsylvania, Dan attended the University of North Carolina at Chapel Hill, where he played football for the Tar Heels. He currently lives happily with his family in Malibu, California.

$INDEX$